DARE TO WRITE

How to confidently write a non-fiction book to grow your business

Steph Caswell

Dare to Write: How to confidently write a non-fiction book to grow your business

First edition (2021)

ISBN: 978-1-7397768-1-7

Published by: Caswell Creative

Cover Design: Ditto Creative

Team Caz, what a journey we've been on!

I can't wait to see what comes next.

TABLE OF CONTENTS

INTRODUCTION

Everybody can be great … because anybody can serve.
You don't have to have a college degree to serve.
You don't have to make your subject and verb agree to serve.
You only need a heart full of grace. A soul generated by love.
Martin Luther King Jr

If you'd told me ten years ago I'd be writing my sixth book, I'd have thought you'd been on the gin. After all, I never aspired to be a writer as a child. It was something that crept up on me, a bit like middle age. But unlike grey hairs or night sweats, writing was a rather welcome surprise. Instead of feeling like a chore, it felt easy and enjoyable. An escape from my busy life as a teacher.

And, like anything, the more I wrote, the better I became. Malcolm Gladwell would be proud. But most importantly, the more I wrote, the more I loved it. And I think *that* was the unexpected part. After all, research shows the more you practise something, the more skilled you become. But to love something too? That's not always guaranteed.

In 2015, I decided to try my hand at writing a book for teachers. It was my bread and butter after all. Over ten years at the chalkface and now a deputy headteacher, I had advice to give to those starting out. So what better way to do it than writing it all in a book? I can't remember the moment I decided to write it, but I can remember feeling a sense of excitement.

The only trouble was I didn't really know how to do it. I sat and tried to type out my thoughts. Every time I'd write a paragraph, I'd reread it and change it, or delete it altogether. I felt incredibly frustrated. In a bid to get a better idea of how best to go about it, I enrolled in Self-Publishing School. I also read everything there was to read about the book writing process and listened to Joanna Penn's *The Creative Penn* podcast. Eventually, my first book came together and I published *Keeping Bums in Seats* on my birthday, 8th June 2015.

Following on from that, I quickly wrote books two and three, publishing them in 2016 and 2017. I also ghost wrote two books for an Australian publisher in the self-development niche. In 2018, I submitted my children's book to the Golden Egg Academy. I was accepted into a cohort of ten writers from almost one hundred applicants and, although I'm still working on my manuscript, I've learned so much. Writing became not only my creative outlet but my job too.

But writing is not universally loved by all. It's often seen as a laborious side of being a business owner, something to outsource where possible. But, for a few of us, writing is an integral part of who we are. It ignites a little fire in our bellies. We begin publishing blog posts regularly or showcasing our skills in social media captions. Suddenly, the idea of publishing a book doesn't seem so crazy.

And the reason? You're passionate about what you do. You have so much knowledge in your area of expertise and you love helping and serving others, building relationships within your community. Working with clients and seeing their achievements gives you a sense of pride. Sharing in client transformations and successes is one of the best things about being a service-based business owner, right?

So now you're ready to share your expertise on a wider scale. And why shouldn't you? Writing a book isn't just for the privileged few anymore. More and more people are achieving publishing success and thriving as a result. Now it's your turn.

And that's where I come in.

Why I wrote this book

Writing a book is no mean feat. It's a journey that leaves you feeling jubilant one minute and ready to gouge your eyes out with a spoon the next. It really is an endeavour like no other.

And it's the sheer enormity of it that puts people off. As the old cliché goes, 'Everyone has a book inside them.' I'm sure they do, but not everyone ends up writing it. Quite often, when people find out I'm an author, they say, 'I've always wanted to write a book.' Quite often, I smile and say, 'What's stopping you?'

Time, confidence and imposter syndrome come up as the most frequent answers. 'I don't have time' or 'I wouldn't know where to start.' Maybe you've uttered these words yourself. And that's okay. It's perfectly normal to feel that way. After all, you've probably read books by some of your personal development heroes and feel hugely under-qualified to be in the same league as them.

But that's where I'm going to stop you.

You're just as qualified to write a book as they are. Don't you think they sat there at some point thinking the same thing? Of course they did. Nobody is born a bestselling author. Everybody starts with a blank page. It's how you fill it that matters. And that's why I wrote this book. Because I want anyone with aspirations to write a book to feel supported. To feel confident they've got what it takes. To grab imposter syndrome by the scruff of the neck and give it a good shake.

To see their name on the front cover and feel a surge of pride at their achievement.

Because that's what it is, a monumental achievement. And one I'm here to support you to achieve, every step of the way.

How to read this book

Not all books need to be read in a linear way, but a book about writing a book does. You can't easily edit a book you haven't written or hit publish on something you've not even started. Everyone has a process for writing and, over the next twelve chapters, I'll be sharing mine with you. I'll take you from your initial idea to publication, touching on the mindset and the habits required to write too.

By the end, you'll have a tried and tested system that works. It's worked for me for each book I've written. But that doesn't mean it's perfect. There's no one-size-fits-all solution to writing a book. Everyone will approach it slightly differently and you may find parts of this book that don't apply directly to your process.

But I would urge you to read the whole thing first. You may feel you've got mindset strategies that work for other parts of your business, but a writer's mindset is something different. Equally, you may feel as though you're great at launching new services and you're really confident to do the same here, but again, do read through the chapter on launching your book, as there are always new ideas to consider.

Once you've read it through, go back and complete each stage in turn. It's always easier to know the direction you're heading, but then to take each part of the journey as it comes. Some parts will take longer than others, but resist the urge to compete with yourself. Just take it a step at a time. Revisit sections of the book as and when you need to.

And finally

I want to wish you the best of luck. What you're about to do is truly remarkable. As I said, so many people say they'd love to write a book, but very few realise that dream. It's easier to say than it is to do.

Throughout the process, be kind to yourself. Like anything challenging, you need to be your biggest cheerleader. Keep reminding yourself of how far you've come and how much you've achieved. If you need time away from your manuscript, take it. But most importantly, surround yourself with people who will support you on your quest.

And remember this one thing, I'm one of those supporters – the Rodney to your Del Boy, the Marge to your Homer, the Thelma to your Louise.

And when you take that leap off the cliff to publication, I'll be right there next to you, screaming on the way down.

If you feel something calling you to dance or write or paint or sing, please refuse to worry about whether you're good enough. Just do it. Be generous. Offer a gift to a world that no one else can offer. Yourself.

Glennon Doyle

CHAPTER 1

WHY WRITE A BOOK?

Whatever makes you uncomfortable is your biggest opportunity.

Bryant McGill

In 2014, in a moment of madness, I decided to run a half marathon. After scouring the internet, I found one at Silverstone, running around the same track as the F1 drivers, but thankfully not at the same time. Training went reasonably well and when race day came around, I felt pretty confident.

So confident in fact that when the race started, I went out a little on the fast side, covering the first 5k in a new PB. I felt like a million bucks. Now, if you know anything about running, you'll realise I'd made a massive mistake. Because when you go out too fast, you hit the dreaded 'wall'. Something I can only describe as running with concrete blocks attached to your feet while hungover. Still not sure? Just type 'Jonny Brownlee hitting the wall' into Google … You're welcome.

When I eventually crossed the finish line after two and a half hours, I burst into tears, sobbing like a drunk teenager on the poor man who was trying to untie the time-tracking chip from my shoelaces. I was incoherent and exhausted. I also became aware of a 'situation' in my left shoe, but with a 90-minute drive home ahead of me, taking my shoes off wasn't an option.

After refuelling with food, crying some more and trying to squat in a Portaloo, I eventually began the journey home. Two hours later, I collapsed on my bed, took a deep breath and removed my shoe. My sock, previously white, was now red. Slowly peeling it off, I realised the gravity of the situation.

Where there once had been a toenail on my second toe, there was now a bloody mess. Five toenails had unglamorously become four. It was gross.

When I reflect back on that day, I feel a mixture of emotions. One being a desire to buy bigger trainers. But the main one is pride. It made me realise I can do hard things, things that seem insurmountable at the time.

And that's how you might feel about writing a book for your business. It's such a huge project, it can feel too overwhelming to even start. And when something feels that way, it's important to understand the benefits of doing it in the first place.

Much like when I planned to run my half marathon, I knew the benefits before I began – raising money for charity, getting fitter and stronger, finally losing some of the sodding baby weight. Yes, I knew the risks too, but to do anything difficult, there have to be benefits as well, right?

Writing a book for your business

You might be wondering why on earth you should write a book to grow your business. And I get that. It's an awfully big project and it's unlikely to be an instant bestseller. It's not something that's going to happen without some blood, sweat and tears too. Hopefully no lost toenails though.

Frankly, it's like running that half marathon. It seems like a good idea at first. But then, when you hit the wall, you instantly regret signing up for the bloody thing in the first place. Not even the temptation of a baby-shaped jelly sweet is going to get you to the finish line.

It's a question I get asked a lot. You've got a successful business, *why* would writing a book help? *How* can it help it grow? Unlike marathon running, where hitting 'the wall', shitting yourself and long-term injury are all possibilities, there are many benefits to writing a book to grow your business.

From reaching a wider audience to becoming the go-to expert in your niche, writing a book opens doors that you didn't even know existed. In this chapter, we're going to dive into just what those doors are and how they can benefit you.

You can even bring some jelly babies along for the ride.

The benefits of writing a book for your business

You might feel speculative about book writing. Maybe it's something you've always thought 'other people' did. Maybe you've tried writing one but gave up when you weren't even sure how to start. And that's okay. Actually, it's more than okay. It's very common. When you know how hard something is, you want to be sure the benefits are worth it. So let's dive in, shall we?

Benefit #1: Wider reach

If you've grown your business via the 1:1 method, or even the 1:few, you're only able to reach a handful of people at any one time. Yes, you may have an email list or a sizeable following on social media, but your followers are only able to access a bite-sized amount of your value at a time.

Packaging your knowledge into a book can give you the wider reach you're seeking. All your knowledge and expertise are in one place. You can help more people – maybe even internationally.

Benefit #2: Increased leads and enquiries

A wider reach means more people are going to be interested in working with you. Whether it's via a digital course, a group programme, or your signature 1:1 offer, your book can open doors to all sorts of enquiries, from all sorts of people.

After writing *Keeping Bums in Seats*, I had enquiries from a national teaching magazine to write regular features and from schools seeking workshops for staff. Neither of which I'd considered before writing it. When I interviewed Sarah Townsend, author of *Survival Skills for Freelancers*, she explained how opportunities have arisen for her that she'd never envisioned either, like mentoring.

Benefit #3: Become an expert in your niche

People love experts. Writing a book instantly raises your profile to expert status. You have expertise in a niche area and, therefore, you become instantly recognisable. Think of the books you've read by experts; no doubt they've changed your life in some way. You can be that person for someone too.

As soon as you're seen as an expert, people want more of you. Whether it's through interviews or consulting, working with an expert has appeal. If Brené Brown offered to work with me on courage and vulnerability, I'd snap that up in a heartbeat. Writing a book is no mean feat and people respect that too.

Benefit #4: PR opportunities

As small business owners, we're often seeking ways to get eyes on our brand, and, more often than not, it's down to us to make connections. Writing a book provides you with plenty of opportunities for that. When approaching podcasters, bloggers or event hosts, having a book to your name can make you a very appealing guest.

And it's not only opportunities in the digital world. Speaking engagements are another possibility for authors. Events are often looking for speakers, and with a book under your belt, you're often seen as a credible source on a topic. It's also a great way to sell copies of your book at an event full of your ideal readers.

Benefit #5: Build out your business model

As a service-based business owner, working with people is your top priority. Whether it's through 1:1 offers or group programmes, you're often working alongside those who are seeking a transformation. Building a book into your business model allows you to diversify and build a passive income stream.

Many successful authors have courses that run alongside their books, either self-led online courses or programmes with live sessions built in, with each chapter of their book becoming a module in the accompanying course. It's also possible to create workshops that accompany your book too. Both of these are models that have worked for me.

Why not look at this from the reverse perspective? If you have a successful course or workshop you currently run, turning it into a book is a great way to add another layer to your sales funnel.

Benefit #6: Self-publishing makes it simpler

It's often said there's never been a better time to publish a book. Gone are the days of exclusivity, with authors being the chosen few who jumped successfully through the hoops of traditional publishing. Self-publishing makes it accessible to everyone.

And while traditional publishing still holds a certain kudos in the writing world, it's not the be all and end all anymore. In fact, some traditionally published authors are going down the self-publishing route because it puts them in greater control … and the royalties are better. As we'll explore later in this book, there are many advantages to publishing your books yourself.

Benefit #7: Increased self-confidence

For me, this is the most important benefit there is. Writing a book is hard. It takes time, effort and a whole lot of drinking gin through a straw. But it's a journey like no other. And when you finally hit 'publish', there's no better feeling. To see your work out there does wonders for your self-belief and self-confidence.

To say you're an author does something to your soul that's hard to explain. You walk a little taller. You smile a little wider. You get a confidence boost that you can take into all other aspects of your life and business. Seeing your name on the front cover and holding your book in your hands is a truly wonderful moment. Don't underestimate it.

Summary

There are so many benefits to writing your book, both professionally and personally. It's hard to get them all down and do them all justice. Believe me when I say the possibilities are endless – and exciting!

Throughout this book we'll explore all these in more detail. By the end, you'll not only know how to write your book, but exactly how it's going to benefit and enhance your business too.

Action steps

1. Write down how you think a book could benefit your business. How could it enhance your business model? Where would it feature in your sales funnel?
2. How could it benefit you personally? How would writing and publishing a book make you feel on a personal level? What are you hoping to experience?
3. Which courses/workshops/masterclasses have you done that you could turn into a book? Just jot these down for now, as we'll explore this in more detail in later chapters.
4. Always wear trainers one size larger when running long distances.

CHAPTER 2

A WRITER'S MINDSET

You have to have the courage to be rubbish to even begin.
Greg McKeown

My sister has a retriever called Goldie. She's six years old and one determined pooch. When Goldie sets her mind to something, she doesn't give up. Ever. Normally this involves a tennis ball and an endless desire to play fetch.

Goldie has always known her own mind. If she's off the lead and gets a scent, she'll stop at nothing to find the source. She's been known to disappear for over half an hour, finally returning without so much as an apologetic sniff, while we're all close to shitting our pants.

One afternoon, my brother-in-law, Aaron, took Goldie for a walk by the river. As many retrievers do, she loves a swim and decided to have a paddle. Unfortunately for Aaron, Goldie picked up a scent and proceeded to do more than paddle. She swam across the width of the river to the other side.

Not only that, she got out and began heading down the towpath. Pandemonium ensued as Aaron tried to communicate with people on the opposite bank to try and catch her. Goldie, however, had no intention of doing as she was told and merrily continued trotting down the path.

Finally, she was caught by a couple, and a man brought her back across the river in his canoe.

Needless to say, Goldie hasn't been allowed off the lead near the river since. I'm not entirely sure Aaron has fully recovered from the experience. Goldie, on the other hand, couldn't give two shits.

So why am I telling you this?

Because you need to have the mindset and determination of Goldie to write a book.

Before you even write a word, get the right head on your shoulders. All your ideas, confidence and determination start in your head. If you don't have the right mindset to write, you're going to struggle.

Simple as that.

Now you might be well-versed in the importance of mindset. Heck, maybe you're even a mindset coach. But this is an opportunity to stop and reflect on your *writer's* mindset. Writing a book is an adventure requiring you to dig deep, often many times over.

So how can you develop a mindset that helps rather than hinders?

Well, I'm glad you asked.

The shitty first draft

> *Shitty First Drafts. All good writers write them.*
> *That is how they end up with good second drafts and terrific third drafts.*
> **Anne Lamott**

Ah, the shitty first draft. One of my favourite parts of the writing process. Why? Because it enables you to go into something without the weight of perfection.

Writing is a marathon, not a sprint. A lot of what you write in your first draft will be shitty, so you must make your peace with that. Author Greg McKeown even goes as far as to call it 'draft zero' - as he knows it's going to be terrible.

It's all about embracing the shit. Embracing the creative journey and all its pit stops. Picasso didn't create his masterpieces with the first brush stroke. Michelangelo didn't create *David* with the first blow of his chisel.

To think you're going to write your best work with the first few strokes of the keyboard is madness. You're putting too much pressure on yourself to get things right the first time.

No one gets their writing right the first time. No one.

So do me a favour, would you? Go into the process knowing you'll suck. Knowing there'll be times when you want to set fire to your manuscript and watch it burn. We've all been there.

The most important thing is to keep going. Don't stop. Embrace the suck.

Your inner critic

Oh, your inner critic loves this kind of project. In fact, it loves it so much it pitches a tent and pops some beers in the fridge. You know that though, right? When you're trying anything new, your inner critic comes to town to set up camp.

Sometimes, your inner critic's opinion can be so strong it stops you in your tracks. You close your laptop, fully convinced this 'writing a book' idea is totally stupid.

But I've got a different take on the inner critic. I like to think it rears its head because it's trying to protect you. Much like a well-meaning aunt when they ask why you're still single; it comes from a place of love.

Writer Elizabeth Gilbert talks about the inner critic in a similar vein. Instead of trying to ignore it or telling it to pipe down, Elizabeth suggests inviting it along for the journey. Imagine it's a companion sitting in the back seat of this experience. Allow it to sit there, but don't let it give you directions or opinions about your 'driving'.

So rather than wasting valuable energy on trying to quieten your inner critic, why not take Elizabeth's stance and invite it along for the ride? Acknowledge its attempts to sabotage your writing, rather than trying to drown it out. Much like your conversation with your aunt, reassure it you're okay. You don't need protection.

Yes, you're nervous about putting your book out there, but you're going to keep going anyway. Remind yourself that all writers/creatives feel this way when completing a project. It's just part of the process. It shouldn't be something that stops you in your tracks.

Limiting beliefs

You've probably heard of limiting beliefs. We've all got them and they can impact us in any aspect of our lives.

But I'm inviting you to specifically consider your limiting beliefs about your writing. Sometimes you carry these beliefs from childhood, particularly if a teacher made you think you were shit at it.

If that's the case, and it's one that comes up often when I'm mentoring, tackle those beliefs head on. Why? Because otherwise they'll eventually stop you writing. Once motivation, excitement and sheer determination have left the building, any limiting beliefs about your writing will bring their overnight bag and join the inner critic for a few drinks.

Let's unpack this a bit. Limiting beliefs are just that – beliefs. When you hear your inner voice telling you you're shit at writing, look for the facts. What evidence do you have to support this? If it's a report from your Year 5 teacher, you can safely remind yourself you've gained many writing skills since then.

If it was a throwaway comment from a colleague or friend (those are just the worst, right?), find evidence to back up their words. Research shows 95–97% of our decisions come through the emotional 'chimp' part of the brain. It's these emotions that hamper our chances.

Look for cold, hard facts. Can't find any? Then crack on! Found a fact that proves you right? Find ways to get support. Writing coaches or courses can help improve your writing skills. Know you're terrible at grammar? That's what editors are for!

As author and speaker Marie Forleo says, 'everything is figureoutable'. Don't let a lack of skills stand in your way. Not in today's digital world, where there's always someone or something to help.

Imposter syndrome

Another brilliant part of being creative, imposter syndrome likes to join the party too, swapping stories with your inner critic and limiting beliefs, toasting your failure.

And just like your inner critic, imposter syndrome often stems from limiting beliefs you hold. But it also comes from a fear of failure and judgement.

Somewhere inside, you're probably hearing these types of questions:

- Who am I to write a book?
- I don't have enough experience, do I?
- Should I do a master's/PhD to seem more credible?
- What if people think I'm a wanker for writing a book?

Our fear of what other people think can be so problematic. We've all read those scathing book reviews, right? You don't want the same thing to happen to you. I get that.

But the problem with taking that view is that you'll never do things you really want to do, like writing a book, skinny dipping or howling at the moon for the heck of it. If people's opinions are always at the forefront of your mind, it stifles your creativity and ambition.

Always remember other people's judgements and opinions come from their own insecurities. Or jealousy. You're doing something they wish they could do and it brings out a case of the green-eyed monster.

If there was a way I could banish your fear with a wave of my magic wand, I would. But instead, try some of these on for size:

- Print off lovely testimonials from clients and stick them up around your writing space – these people are your supporters and they'll be an integral part of your writing journey.
- Find inspirational quotes about perseverance or managing fear to keep you feeling motivated.
- Select some positive mantras you can say to yourself when you feel imposter syndrome calling – interrupt negative thinking with something positive.

One thing I always try to remember is you don't have to be an expert to write a book. You don't need a PhD for people to take your work seriously. If you can speak to people in a way that resonates, if you can empathise with them and show them the transformation they seek, your true fans won't care. PhD or not, you're giving them skills, knowledge and experiences to really help them.

Do I have a PhD in teaching? Absolutely not. But I *am* more experienced than teachers just starting out. Do I have a master's in writing? Nope. But I *have* studied it for ten years. I've written close to half a million words in various different ways. I've written six books.

It all adds up. But most importantly, I can empathise with you, the reader. A master's degree doesn't do that. It'll give me a huge hole in my bank balance, but it won't give me empathy or make up for my years of learning and experience. It's a great thing to have, but it's not a necessity.

You only have to be a few stages further along the journey than your reader to provide valuable information. Your experiences and your knowledge up to this point are just what they're seeking.

So stop worrying about credentials and start thinking about all the people you can help.

Growth vs fixed mindset

> *In a growth mindset, challenges are exciting rather than threatening. So rather than thinking, 'Oh I'm going to reveal my weaknesses', you say, 'Wow! Here's a chance to grow.'*
>
> **Carol Dweck**

Changing your mindset can have a profound impact on every aspect of your life, not just your writing. But it can transform your writing experience in so many different ways too.

Understanding the difference between a fixed and growth mindset is helpful when considering how to tackle the writing process. It's also important in relation to how you perceive your book's success.

Coming into the writing process with a fixed mindset is often characterised by assuming your ability to write is set in stone. You'll only be able to write to a certain level. It's here where you may begin to question if you have the ability to write at all. That other people must be 'more talented' than you. That you're not a natural writer.

I've been there too. But do you honestly believe I was born a writer? That I requested a notebook and pen from the midwife at the moment of my birth? Of course not. My ability to write has come from years of practice, from constantly learning about the craft and by reading.

It's come from trying and failing many times. From screwing up so many ideas and throwing them in the bin so many times I've lost count. From writing tens of thousands of words that won't ever see the light of day.

That's a growth mindset. Knowing talent and ability isn't fixed. Knowing practice and the willingness to fail many times over will get you to where you want to be. How arrogant would you have to be to think you're a naturally gifted writer who never has to put the hours in? I'm not suggesting you're like that. But there are people out there who are.

So, as I said earlier, embrace the journey and the learning along the way. Go into this process with the mindset for growth. You won't like everything you write. You may question yourself over and over again about whether this is the right decision. You may analyse every little mistake.

But mistakes are how we learn. I wouldn't have written six books without making a ton of them. So choose a growth mindset over a fixed one. Choose curiosity over analysis. It'll make the writing process so much more enjoyable.

Writer's block

Ah, writer's block. Does it exist or not? The jury's out on that one. Seen as a curse or a disease on many unsuspecting writers, it's often a fancy way of describing procrastination. Something we all have experience of in one way or another.

The cure? Well, as much as I'd love to give you a potion to drink, it actually comes down to one thing. Action. Procrastination absolutely hates it when you take decisive action. So, as tempting as it is to redesign the kitchen cupboards or laminate the floor, the only way to take control of the 'block' is to power on through.

It's perception. Perception of the task ahead and how well you think you can tackle it. When you think of writing a whole book, the process becomes daunting. Breaking it down into chunks is the only way to tackle it and ensure your action is consistent.

People may advocate writing when you feel like it, but I advise caution here. As author Jack London said, 'You can't wait for inspiration. You have to go after it with a club.' Don't wait for the muse or the moment to take you. It won't. Only consistent action will encourage it to come out of hiding.

In the next chapter, we'll look at habits and systems you can put in place to write consistently. Developing these habits will defeat writer's block. But there's one trick I've learned that can really help you with any form of procrastination. It's a concept that's been fully explored and developed by Mel Robbins in her book *The 5 Second Rule.*

It's about interrupting the five seconds between when you think about doing something and when your emotional brain kicks in and talks you out of it. As soon as you sit down to write, count back from five to zero and then go! Just start typing or planning or editing. It's such a powerful technique for defeating procrastination and has worked for me on so many occasions.

Finding your voice

Often, aspiring writers worry about finding their authentic voice. So much so it stops them writing at all, fearing they must know their voice before they write.

But you'll only develop your authentic voice through practice. Through free writing, journalling or blogging, even through writing social media captions. It's not something you know without trying. And, to be honest, it often mirrors your actual voice.

I'm a sarcastic Sally and so that seeps its way into my writing. I take the piss and enjoy a good laugh, so again this is evident in my author 'voice'.

But I've only realised that through practice. And with practice comes confidence.

Remember, writing is a skill. You wouldn't sign up for a marathon and show up at the start line without any training, would you? It's the same with writing. You have to practise. So why not have fun with it? Free writing is a great way to do this and there are many prompts online to help you.

Please don't spend time worrying about finding your voice. It's there. It always has been. Now's the time to sit down and use it.

Summary

Mindset really is the key to becoming a successful writer. Yes, you need certain skills to be successful, but unless you have the confidence and determination to sit down and write each day, all those skills will go to waste.

Leave your limiting beliefs in the past; they won't serve you during this process. Consider the questions you would ask your clients about limiting beliefs. Use them to challenge your own inner critic or imposter syndrome. Often these are useful free writing or journalling prompts.

It's so important to embrace the journey. To have high expectations of yourself, but not so gargantuan that they stop you even starting. Enjoy the process. Use it as a learning experience and accept there'll be bumps along the way. It's the only way to do it.

But most importantly, be kind to yourself. How we speak to ourselves is often never the way we'd speak to loved ones. Catch your negative chatter and practise turning it on its head and finding the positives instead. Give yourself the same encouragement you'd give your best friend if they were struggling.

It really can make all the difference.

Action steps

1. Practise 'free writing' or journalling – have fun with your creativity and see where it takes you. You'll find plenty of prompts online to help you.
2. When you're struggling with procrastination, try the 'five-second rule' – it can help you just get started.
3. Read *The 5 Second Rule* by Mel Robbins.
4. Write down your limiting beliefs about writing. Against each belief, write down the facts you have to support it. If you find none, use some affirmations to help turn those negative thoughts into positive ones. If you can find facts, what could you do to improve your skills?
5. Keep your dog on a lead near a river.

CHAPTER 3

HABITS AND PRODUCTIVITY

First forget inspiration. Habit is more dependable. Habit will sustain you whether you're inspired or not.

Octavia Butler

Stephen King writes 2,000 words a day, come rain or shine. Even on Christmas Day and his birthday, he's at his desk and doesn't leave until he's achieved his word count.

Victor Hugo had a slightly different approach. He stripped naked and had his clothes locked away, so he wouldn't leave the house until he'd written his book.

Two different authors, two wildly different sets of writing habits. While sometimes quirky or downright bizarre, the most successful writers thrive on good habits.

But should you strive to have the *same* writing habits as your author heroes? Should you, like Victor Hugo, sit with your bits out in order to get the words on the page?

Thankfully, no.

The power of habits

Habits are an integral part of your life. They bring a level of automaticity to your daily routines to give your brain a chance to conserve energy. If you actively thought about every single repetitive action you ever did, you'd be exhausted before you'd even got dressed in the morning.

Developing consistent writing habits is the key to taking your idea and turning it into a book. Your habits will help you when you've lost motivation or have reached the soggy middle of a book, which often feels like wading through golden syrup while wearing flippers. But enough about my weekend ...

Without consistent habits, you'll struggle to get your book finished.

Everyone responds differently to outer and inner expectations. We've all been there on New Year's Eve, pledging a new way of life for the following year, only to see our best intentions crumble into the nearest packet of custard creams. Later in this chapter, you can discover how your personality type impacts your ability to create and stick to new habits.

You'll also discover some simple techniques to help you create manageable habits that fit into your lifestyle. You're a business owner after all, so you're often battling against the many other elements of running a business. You're also trying to maintain some sense of a work-life balance, which is incredibly important.

Building successful habits

According to the *Cambridge English Dictionary*, a habit is 'something you do often and regularly, sometimes without knowing you are doing it'. A bit like putting the same leg into your trousers first or taking the same route to work each day.

When it comes to building new habits, the easier you can make your new habit, the better. In his book *Tiny Habits*, BJ Fogg encourages his readers to make any new, potentially difficult habit into something small and stupidly easy.

Fogg took this to another level when trying to implement a habit of completing push-ups each day. After every visit to the toilet, he'd complete two push-ups. Just two. His reason? If he made the new habit almost too easy, he'd be more inclined to do it. And it worked.

But Fogg also found that he often felt like doing more than two push-ups. Sometimes he completed five or eight or ten. As long as he did a minimum of two, anything else was a bonus. He also did the same thing with flossing his teeth. He set himself the easy goal of flossing one tooth, safe in the knowledge that once he'd done one, he'd be more inclined to do the rest.

And that's the beauty of the *Tiny Habits* philosophy. Often with new habits/behaviours, it's getting started that requires the most effort. Author Darren Hardy compares it to starting the roundabout at a children's play area. It takes a lot of effort to get the thing moving but once momentum builds, it takes on a life of its own.

By making the initial 'push' easier, you're more likely to complete the new habit, thus building the neural pathways in the brain associated with behaviour change.

When creating a new behaviour, like a writing habit, Fogg follows a basic formula:

Behaviour = Motivation + Ability + Prompt (B = MAP)

Surprisingly, Fogg's research has shown motivation is the last thing you should rely on when building new writing habits. It's unreliable and fleeting. Creating the ability to complete your new habit, backed up by a useful prompt, is really the answer to being successful.

Your ability to build new writing habits

A new habit often feels exciting. You're pumped and ready for action. If you're set on taking up running, you'll buy new running shoes and some fancy socks. If you're keen to start writing regularly, you'll get a fancy new notebook and maybe even a snazzy pen or two.

For the first few days, you're a keen bean. You show up for your writing slot like an athlete at the Olympic 100m final. Maybe you even slap your thighs to get the blood pumping and do a few star jumps. You close your eyes and visualise your book in the hands of your readers. TED talk, here you come.

But after a few days or even weeks, when you sit down to write, the novelty has well and truly worn off. Instead of an Olympic athlete, you're now approaching your writing sessions like one of those racehorses reluctant to get into the starting gate. You begin to put them off, telling yourself you'll get back into the swing of things *soon*. Before you know it, you haven't written for weeks and your book now seems like a distant dream.

But there's an easier way! By improving your ability to complete your new writing habit, you can get past procrastination or lack of motivation. Remember, the easier you make the habit, the more likely you are to complete it.

Start by creating a tiny word-count target that seems almost ridiculous. Really. Something that when you think about it seems almost laughable. Something you'd be embarrassed to even tell the dog about.

Here's an example. Set yourself a target of writing just fifty words each day. The likelihood is that once you've got the 'roundabout' moving, you'll carry on writing past your fifty words and onto a sizeable chunk of writing. And if you don't? If you just write fifty words? Well, you've still hit your word-count target and made progress with your book.

Because the simpler the new habit, the more likely you are to do it every day. Often, people set out with the best intentions, claiming they're going to write for two hours a day. But after only a few days, they're exhausted and willing to lose their laptop in a freak accident with a hammer.

You'll recognise this if you've ever tried to take up running or cut out carbs in January. You last on willpower for a little while, but eventually it's just too hard. You give up and have that sense of self-loathing when you try to pull on your pre-Christmas jeans. Your inner critic pops back for a visit, whispering to your imposter syndrome about your flabby bits.

But setting tiny, seemingly insignificant steps, like fifty words a day, will get you closer to finishing your book. Some days it may be twenty words, but other days it could be two thousand. You're able to achieve success on a daily basis and it'll do your self-confidence a world of good. You feel motivated to continue.

Just like BJ's post-pee push-ups, you'll soon be writing on a consistent basis and feeling fantastic.

Setting up habit prompts

As well as improving your ability to complete your new habit, you can also use prompts to help you complete it. Again, we often start with good intentions. You might even be wondering why on earth you'd need a prompt to help you. It's unlikely you'll forget to do your new habit, right?

Sadly it comes down to a change in priority. When you start a new habit, it's often the main focus of your day. Motivation is in town and you wake up with feelings of excitement and anticipation. If you're anything like me, you'll start this new habit on a Monday, to begin the week as you mean to go on.

However, once you've done your new habit for a while, it's no longer your top priority. Especially if it's time-consuming or hard to complete. Other things happen to push this new habit out of your day and into … never. You forget to do it or tell yourself you'll do it later, but later never comes.

BJ Fogg suggests using prompts to help you continue your habit. A prompt can be visual or auditory. It might be an alarm on your phone telling you it's time to do your tiny habit. It could be the visual prompt of leaving your laptop and notebook out, so it's the first thing you see when you get to your desk each day.

Coupled together with a tiny habit that's simple to do, habit prompts help you establish consistency. By giving your brain a quick prompt, you'll find you don't miss out on completing your new writing habit and, eventually, completing the habit becomes automatic.

Creating familiarity for your brain

One other way to help your brain implement new habits is to create a sense of familiarity. Our brains are very good at linking certain behaviours to certain environments. In the world of writing habits, this could look like:

- Sitting in the same place to write each day
- Wearing the same cardigan when you write
- Listening to the same playlist of music each time you write

But why would you want to do this? Surely it can't make that much difference? Actually it can. If your brain hears the same piece of music every time you sit down to write, it'll associate it with the writing process.

When I interviewed author Jacqueline Kent on 'Happy Writers Live!', she agreed with this idea. Not only did she have the same playlist for every writing session, she also had a bowl of sweets to accompany each session. Jelly baby, anyone?

Whatever you can do to make your writing experience simple and familiar for your brain, the better. Before you tackle your word count each day, get into your writing zone, both physically and mentally. It really helps with creativity. You may prefer to write in silence in a quiet corner of the house. Or you may enjoy writing in your local coffee shop, surrounded by background noises such as chatting or the whirr of machines. Stephen King writes while listening to Metallica.

It comes down to personal preference. And if writing in a coffee shop eats into your bank balance, you can play coffee shop noises via YouTube in the comfort of your own home.

A word of warning though! Don't get too particular about having everything 'just right' when writing. Aspiring to be Goldilocks in any situation is often procrastination in disguise. While your writing environment should be comfortable and give your brain a sense of familiarity, don't spend too much time getting everything together.

Decide where you feel comfortable writing, create that space, gather your accessories and get started!

Accountability

When creating any new habit, accountability plays an important role for many people. Unless you are one of the small percentage of people who readily meets inner and outer expectations without any level of accountability, you'll need to set something up.

What that accountability looks like is up to you. Some people prefer having an accountability buddy. Someone you can send your daily or weekly word count to. Others prefer the group approach and the camaraderie that goes with it.

Social media is full of these types of writing groups. I belong to a couple that give me motivation to write my children's book. I particularly enjoy the writing 'sprints' each day, where groups of writers get together virtually to dedicate an hour to writing. You'd be surprised at how motivating it is just to turn up and put your writing first.

It's not about sharing your word count or where you're up to either; it's simply about showing up and dedicating time to write. If you'd like to join one, why not become part of The Happy Writers' Club? My Facebook group which supports non-fiction writers to write their books.

But if you're more introverted and working with an accountability partner/group doesn't appeal, you can hold yourself accountable in other ways. I used the 'writing sprint' technique to write the very words you're reading. Setting aside blocks of time each day to write and protecting those blocks as an appointment with myself I couldn't miss.

Another way that's worked for me in the past is to use an old-fashioned wall calendar. Each day, I logged my word count so I could see my progress in a very visual way. Hanging it on my wall near my writing desk made it part of my writing zone and motivated me to continue. For this book I used a spreadsheet to log my word count and that worked too.

If you're feeling really brave, you can even share your word count on social media. Accountability, but from a safe distance! This was another technique I used when writing this book, as I wanted to bring my audience on the writing journey with me.

Your support network

Writing is a lonely business for most of us. It's not often you're part of a group of writers working on a project, and even if you are, you still have to have the discipline to write your bit. To get past the loneliness factor, you need to find your support crew. A group of people you trust to support you as you embark on this adventure.

When your inner critic kicks in or you feel a dip in motivation, having people to cheer you on is so important. But who will be part of your crew? You might feel embarrassed to share your writing aspirations with people, but I can honestly say I've only ever had positive feedback.

If you're careful with who you select, you'll know the response you're likely to receive. Telling your supportive friend who is only going to encourage you and spur you on is very different from telling your cynical neighbour who will just tell you how hard it's going to be.

You don't need a team as large as Beyoncé's either, just a few people you can turn to. Try and pick people who fall into these categories:

- The Listener – someone to listen as you tell them how things are going, asking a few questions here and there to further their understanding, but are purely there as a sounding board.
- The Bum-Kicker – a friend who won't listen to your bullshit. When you tell them you don't think you'll ever finish this book or it's too hard, they'll tell you to pull your finger out and keep going. All from a place of love, of course!
- The Cheerleader – a member of your crew who'll tell you how brilliant and inspiring you are. Not someone who's got their head up your arse, but who knows positivity and enthusiasm matter. Someone who'll buy a copy of your book for all their friends and shout about it from the rooftops.
- The Wise Owl – someone who's done something challenging before – maybe they've even written their own book. They know the highs and lows of challenges. They know the bumpy journey better than anyone. You'd call on them for sound advice and a few tips to get you through.

You might not have all of these people in your life, but don't worry. Sometimes just one or two friends will do. But don't try to do this alone if you can help it.

Summary

Building consistent yet manageable writing habits is the key to success. But while I can give you suggestions and tips, how you build these habits is up to you. You may feel as though daily writing is for you, or you may feel irritated at the suggestion of such a strict regime.

If you're struggling with establishing good writing habits, avoid berating yourself. The *Tiny Habits* philosophy advocates keeping things small and simple. If you're still struggling to fit in your writing time, look at how you could make things even tinier. It's not about the number of words you write, not really. It's about showing up. By consistently finding even ten minutes of writing time, you're proving to yourself you're serious about getting your book out there.

Ask yourself, 'What would my writing habits look like if they were easy?' Or, in the words of author Greg McKeown, 'What would they look like if they were effortless?'

There are no prizes for slogging your guts out. There are only prizes for finishing and publishing. And even then, the prize could simply be a slice of cake and a cuppa with your support crew. Just take it one step at a time. One day at a time. One word at a time.

Before you know it, all those words will give you a finished book. And there's no greater feeling.

Action steps

1. Decide on the writing habits you want to implement – make them as tiny as you need to.
2. Set up prompts to remind you to complete your new habit.

3. Find your support crew and use them throughout the writing process.
4. Join a writing group for regular support from those in a similar position to you.
5. How could you hold yourself accountable? Use ways that feel right for your personality.
6. Sit with your bits out if it makes you happy. I'm not here to judge ...

CHAPTER 4

YOUR VISION

A vision is not just a picture of what could be; it is an appeal to our better selves, a call to become something more.

Rosabeth Moss Kanter

In late 2014, I was an unhappy deputy headteacher. I'd well and truly fallen out of love with my job and the stress was taking its toll. One afternoon, I attended a meeting about a child who was at risk of being removed from their parents' care. Both parents were addicts and their children were victims of neglect. It was a very sad situation.

At the meeting, the child's mother became very angry, shouting at all the professionals who had gathered together. After I'd given my report about how her child's behaviour had deteriorated in recent months, she turned on me and launched a tirade of verbal abuse, swearing and shouting without holding back.

It was the straw that broke the camel's back.

The months of stress and overwhelm finally came to a head. I didn't return to work for a month, signed off with anxiety and put on medication. As part of my recovery, I decided to read more about meditation and visualisation. Not only did I want to aid my recuperation, I also wanted out. Out of teaching and into something new.

I began to do a morning meditation and visualisation practice I'd read about in *The Miracle Morning* by Hal Elrod. My visualisation consisted of two major things: working for myself and owning a dog. In my head, I visualised writing every day in a cabin at the bottom of my garden with a dog at my feet. Neither of those things existed but I was clear in my mind. This is what I wanted.

Over the months ahead, I began to turn this image into a reality. In January 2015, I resigned from my position as deputy head. In September, I began working part-time as a support teacher.

In March 2016, we brought home our beautiful dog, Flo, and in August we took delivery of our garden cabin. In September 2016, I started my own tutoring and writing business. I finally had everything I'd visualised. What once had started out as an image in my head was now in my back garden.

I'm not telling you this for any other reason than to impress upon you the importance of having a vision. Whether it's for big changes in your life or for smaller ones, like writing your first book.

Now, it might sound grandiose to have a 'vision' for your book. But writing a book is mentally tough. So, like any challenge, it's important to have a game plan. To know where you're heading and what you hope to achieve.

Without this vision in mind, you'll often feel a little flat. Creating it will give you the motivation you need to make friends with the shitty first draft. You can come back to your vision when you feel as though you want to give up. Not only that, when people ask you about your book, you'll have a much clearer picture in your head of what you're writing about and why.

In this chapter, you're going to dig deep and unlock your vision for your book. We're going to cover the key points to consider before you even start typing. Important things such as deadlines and publication dates, as well as professional support and publishing options. We'll also cover the most important aspect: why you're writing this book in the first place.

The 5 Ws of book planning

Before you plan the content of your book in any detail, you need to create an umbrella plan. This acts as an overarching guide to help you write a book your ideal reader wants to read. Without it, you may lose direction and focus. It's a useful plan to come back to during the writing process to stay on target.

But what do the 5 Ws stand for?

- Who – time to discover your ideal reader
- What – the theme of your book and what you're writing about
- Why – one of the most important parts of the planning process – why are you writing *this* particular book?
- When – time to set some deadlines and milestones
- Where – deciding where/how you'll publish your book to know the direction you're going

All of these are such an important part of the whole process. Don't underestimate how confident you'll feel when you've put this umbrella plan together. So let's look at each of them in more detail, shall we?

Who

As a business owner, you've probably done some 'ideal client' work when creating your products or services, getting into the minds of prospective buyers and creating stuff that appeals to them.

It's a similar process when considering your ideal reader (IR). Knowing them inside out is essential to writing a book that appeals to them. You may already know them in part, as they're often people who are/have been clients, or it may be a journey you've been on yourself.

Whatever the situation, there are some useful questions you can ask yourself to help with this part of the planning process. And while demographics help, it's the psychographics that get you under the skin of your reader. Here are a few questions to help you:

- Why is your reader picking up your book?
- What are they searching for? Answers, new knowledge, transformation?
- What challenge(s) are they facing that your book could help them overcome?
- How are they feeling at the start of your book?
- How do they want to feel at the end? How do *you* want them to feel?
- What keeps them up at night?

Often in transformational work, you consider where your client is and where they want to be. Consider your book as the bridge between these two places, guiding your reader on the journey.

You might find it useful to find an image that represents your ideal reader and stick it up in your writing space. It can help you remember to write to one person. If you try to write to everyone, you'll end up writing to no one.

When writing my first book on behaviour management, I got very clear on the demographics and psychographics of my ideal reader:

DEMOGRAPHICS: early twenties, just finished university, single, on a starting salary for teachers, still living at home, newly qualified as a primary school teacher, etc.

PSYCHOGRAPHICS: nervous about managing behaviour, keeps having dreams that the class will run riot, didn't have positive feedback on their behaviour management during their placements, wants to start as they mean to go on, etc.

Now, not everyone who picks up my book will fall into these categories. But think of it like a dart board. Your ideal reader is the bullseye. Most will match your IR description. Other people may buy your book who don't quite hit the target but are on the periphery of your metaphorical board. Most of what you're saying will work for them. A newly qualified secondary school teacher may pick my book up and still get something from it, even though they're not my bullseye reader.

So get specific on who you're writing for.

What

Now this might seem a ridiculous thing to plan for. You're probably already pretty aware of the theme or topic of your book. But it's worth digging a little deeper. Really looking at your niche to ensure it isn't too broad or too narrow.

To be fair, it's quite difficult to become too narrow. Often, the more narrow your book topic, the better. People like to read things in detail. When you think about search terms on Google, you tend to be pretty specific in what you're seeking information about. It's the only way to get the answer you need.

If you're too broad with your niche topic, you won't cover anything in particular detail. There's nothing worse for a reader than reading something that is a bit wishy-washy, where the author has clearly tried to cram in too much information about too many aspects of a niche.

When I first thought about writing a book for early career teachers (ECTs), I realised it's a huge topic – and terribly broad. From behaviour management and managing parents, to teacher wellbeing and managing time, there were so many different aspects I had to cover.

It was then I realised something. If I tried to cover all those huge topics in one book, it wouldn't do them justice. I would probably dedicate a chapter to each, therefore only skimming the surface of the issues at hand. So I decided to look at the topics within the broad niche of being an ECT and create separate books on some of the biggest themes.

Yes, the books were shorter (30,000 words rather than 50,000) but I wanted to address each individual theme, rather than simply mention them in passing.

Instead of one book, I had a series. And I felt as though my readers would get so much more from the experience by doing it this way.

So it's worth looking at your book idea and thinking about how big the topic is. Can you trim it down into something tighter and more detailed so your reader comes away feeling satisfied?

Why

My favourite part of the 5 W approach to planning - finding the real reason for writing your book.

Often people tend to get a bit sheepish when you ask them. They give the very obvious reason of wanting to help people or because they want it as part of their sales funnel.

Neither of these are bad reasons. In fact, both can be part of your 'why'. But I'm going to be frank with you now. You need to go deeper than this. Helping people is all well and good, but when you're sitting in front of the laptop yet again and trying not to weep into your coffee, you'll need something a bit better than that. It needs to be something that is buried deep in your core.

Often it's for a reason that seems a little egotistical. You want to see your name on the cover or you want to start a speaking career. Maybe it's even deeper than that. Maybe it's to prove your English teacher wrong or a critical family member who said you'd never be able to do it.

For me, writing my children's book comes from a place of desire and pride. A desire to see my book on the shelf in my local book shop. When I visualise it among other authors I admire, I feel a flurry of butterflies in my stomach. When I imagine telling people I'm a published children's author, my heartbeat quickens a little.

But my real 'why' is all about making my family proud, showing my children you can achieve anything if you work hard enough and persevere. I want them to feel proud of their old mum and I want to feel proud of myself.

It's that imagery in my head that keeps me writing, even when it's hard.

Your why is a personal thing and will look different to mine. You might not want to share it with others. But as long as you know it yourself, that's all that matters.

When

Now we get to the nitty gritty. We stop thinking in words and start thinking in numbers. Setting deadlines and milestones is crucial for taking your book from just an idea to a fully fledged book. So get your calculator out, find your diary and start making plans.

If you're writing your book to self-publish it, you're not going to have a publishing house or editor breathing down your neck, providing you with deadlines. You're going to have to create your own. Without a deadline, the book writing process can take years rather than months. It's time to get serious about a potential publication date.

It's hard to imagine a publication date before you've even started writing but, as with any goal, it's crucial to success. It's also an excellent starting point to work out your daily word counts to get you to that goal. But how do you set a date and how far into the future should it be?

Ultimately, it depends on you. You know how much time you have to dedicate to writing each day or week. But it needs to feel comfortable for you. It needs to feel manageable but also stretch you a little bit. It's perfectly reasonable to assume that you could write your book in twelve weeks. But it's not just time dependent. It also depends on how long your book is going to be.

An average non-fiction book, traditionally published, is 50,000–75,000 words. If you're self-publishing, however, things get a little more flexible. Essentially, the choice is yours. There's no 'right' number of words. I've read fantastic books that are 10,000 words long. I've also read some brilliant ones closer to 75,000. My three books were 30,000 words each. When starting this one, I gave myself a similar target.

As an example, let's assume you're self-publishing and can write your book in ten weeks. For mathematical ease, it's going to be 30,000-words long.

1. Find a date in ten weeks as a target to complete your draft – make a note of it. Put it up on a sticky note in your writing area so you keep it in mind.
2. If the book is 30,000-words long and you have ten weeks, you'll need to write 3,000 words per week.
3. Decide how many days per week you'll commit to writing. Let's say it's five days per week. You'll therefore need to write 600 words per day.
4. Now things appear far more manageable – you could split your writing into two writing 'sprints' per day, where you just need to write 300 words. Something easily done in thirty minutes.

Suddenly, this behemoth of a writing goal becomes far more manageable. It's not a 30,000-word book you need to think about. It's just writing 600 words per day, five days per week. When you do that on a consistent basis, your 30,000 words will get written in no time. Well, ten weeks … but you catch my drift.

Milestones and rewards

Even though relying on motivation isn't the best way to establish new habits, you can use it to your advantage with your daily word count. Try these to help you:

- Log your word count each day – either on a spreadsheet or on a wall calendar. It's so satisfying to watch your progress grow incrementally, day by day. If you're splitting your writing into two or three 'sprints' each day, you can log each sprint too.
- Set aside milestone markers and rewards – why wait until you've reached the end to feel proud? In his *Tiny Habits* research, BJ Fogg highlights the importance of rewards and celebration to keep new habits in place. I set aside rewards for every 10,000 words. It gives me a little boost to celebrate those milestones.

You can set your milestone markers to be anything that makes you happy. Again, there's no right or wrong. The type of reward is up to you. For me, it might be my favourite chocolate bar or a day away from the writing desk. As long as I know I'll be straight back there tomorrow, there's no harm in taking a day to recover and recharge.

Where

The world of publishing has changed so much in the last decade. It was once reserved for the special few who managed to get past the gatekeepers in traditional publishing. Many aspiring writers had to get used to facing rejection, time and time again. It's still like that in the world of traditional publishing, but the introduction of self-publishing on Amazon changed a lot of things for a lot of people.

Let's compare the two.

Traditional publishing

Traditional publishing has a certain kudos to it that's unlikely to ever go away. It's really the only way to get onto bestseller/awards lists and be easily stocked in bookshops.

To be traditionally published, you can approach a publishing house directly. You might want to approach an agent first, who would then try to find a home for your book with a publisher, particularly if it's one of the bigger publishing houses. With smaller publishers, you may be able to approach them yourself. Quite often, a publisher's website will have information about submissions, telling you exactly what you need to do.

A traditional publisher buys a concept. You don't need a finished book to send in a submission. What you will need is a detailed outline of your book idea so the publisher understands exactly what you're offering. Lots of things will contribute to their decision, including whether they've already got something similar on their list or whether they're currently accepting new authors. It's not always about you.

Understandably, people take rejections personally. But it's important to go into the process knowing you're more likely to hear plenty of 'no thank yous' before you hear a yes. It's just the nature of the beast. If your book submission is accepted, you'll be paid an advance to secure the rights. For a new author, this might only be £5,000. If you have a master's or PhD in a certain subject, that may help you, but not always.

Pros and cons of traditional publishing

Pros:

- Kudos
- Support from the in-house editor, marketing and sales teams
- Being able to walk into a shop and buy your book off the shelf
- Award nominations and bestseller lists

Cons:

- Royalties are lower (only 10% of the cover price)
- You won't see your royalties until you've paid back your advance
- It's likely you'll need a substantial audience for a publisher to be interested in your work – they want people with ready-made buyers!
- From initial enquiry to seeing your book on the shelf can take eighteen months to two years

Self-publishing

Once looked upon as the drunk cousin at traditional publishing's wedding, self-publishing has grown in popularity and authority. In the early days, self-publishing had a bad reputation, thanks to people who published anything and everything, without the support and guidance of professionals.

Over time, however, those who self-publish have worked hard to move away from this reputation. Working with professional editors, proofreaders and cover designers means it's quite hard to tell if a book has been traditionally or self-published. If self-publishing is done well, the only real way to tell is by looking at whether a traditional publisher is named on the inside cover! And there's nothing stopping you creating your own publishing name either.

Self-publishing has never been easier. You can write your book, publish it on any of the digital platforms and have it in the hands of your readers within hours. You start to collect your first royalties sixty days after publishing. There's no advance to pay back or hoops to jump through.

Just bear in mind you'll need to get in with an editor early, as they get booked up weeks or even months in advance. You don't want to be in a position where you've finished your book, but you're having to wait months for editing. More information on this in Chapter 10.

Self-publishing means you're also in full control of your publishing experience. Something traditionally published authors often crave. You decide when the book will be published and where. Amazon is the obvious choice for many, but there's also Kobo, Apple Books, Draft2Digital and IngramSpark. Not only that, you can use drop-shipping to create physical copies of your book or record an audio version too. The possibilities are vast.

Pros and cons of self-publishing

Pros:

- Greater control over when you publish, including subsequent books
- Better royalties (70% for books up to £9.99)
- You decide on the cover design and marketing strategy
- Working with/supporting other small businesses, e.g. editors, designers etc.

Cons:

- The process is entirely your responsibility – writing, publishing, marketing and PR
- Budgeting for an editor, proofreader etc.
- You're accountable – there are no external expectations to get it finished by a particular deadline

- It's difficult to get your book into book shops or onto any bestseller lists

Where and how you publish is entirely up to you. I love the self-publishing option for small business owners, as it's a fairly straightforward process. And I love the fact you can bring your audience on the journey too.

But don't be put off approaching a traditional publisher if that's where your heart lies. It's not impossible. As long as you're ready for the journey ahead, traditional publishing can be an excellent way to get your work out into the world.

Research what's out there

Now you've completed your umbrella plan, you now need to do some research for further information about the marketplace. You won't be surprised to learn your book won't be the only one in its niche. So it's time to get familiar with what else is out there. I don't particularly like the word 'competition', as it suggests you're about to enter the gladiatorial arena, so let's use the word 'community' instead. What else has been published in your niche by other authors in your community?

Here's where Amazon is really useful. It acts as a search engine after all, so use this to your advantage. Fire up your laptop, grab a notebook and pen, and let the research commence!

Here are a few questions/options to consider:

- What other books are out there in your niche? Where would your book be positioned? If you're thinking about traditional publishing, this is a question they're likely to ask.
- Imagine you're in a book shop, which books/authors would sit on either side of your book? It doesn't matter if they're international bestsellers; it's just good to get a picture in your head.

- What do you notice about the bestsellers? Are they just by the 'big names' or are others in there? Read the synopsis and get an idea of what they're offering.
- Look at the 3* or 4* reviews – these are the best ones to focus on. The 5* reviews are great, but they can also trigger imposter syndrome; 1* reviews tend to be written by people who hate life. The 3* and 4* reviews are where the treasure is buried. It's here you'll find what people enjoyed, but also what they were hoping for that the book didn't deliver.

The great thing about this type of research is it gives you a clear idea of where your book belongs. You're also able to use the information to inform the content of your book. By finding out what people were hoping for, but didn't get from other books, you can be sure to include this in your work.

Amazon is a great place for research, but there's also Goodreads, mainly for reviews. You could also poll your audience on social media and see which books they've enjoyed within your niche, giving you further research material.

Summary

You may be keen to just get started with your writing, but this umbrella planning stage is an important part of the process. Don't skip it. Having a vision for your book will help you in many ways and keep you focused on where you're going with this project.

Finally, read widely in your niche to get a clear idea of what other authors are producing in your community. It's so helpful to see how other people have approached your particular topic. Obviously you're not doing this to steal ideas, but there's no harm in reading the work of others. It's often interesting to see a different angle on something you know a lot about.

Don't feel intimidated by doing this either. Avoid comparing yourself to what other people have produced. People will buy your book because *you* wrote it. If imposter syndrome comes to stay, remind yourself that the books you're reading have been thoroughly edited and polished prior to publication. Even the best books out there were shitty first drafts at some point.

But don't restrict your reading to just within your niche area. Try to read lots of non-fiction books. You'll learn so much about how different authors have set them out or what you like or dislike about a particular style. You'll find some you love and some you don't. Reflect on this and make some notes about features you might want to include in your book ... and things you definitely don't want to do.

The best writers are avid readers; it's impossible to absorb good quality work and not let it have a positive impact on your own writing. So which books will you read next?

Action steps

1. Set a target publication date – it doesn't have to be set in stone, but it's good to have something to aim for.
2. Set a target date to finish your first draft – work backwards from your publication date. It could be 4–6 weeks between finishing your first draft, going through the editing process and getting it ready for publication.
3. Decide on a target total word count and set your daily word count, using the formula outlined earlier in the chapter.
4. Look at other books in your niche on Amazon – complete the research suggested to give you a solid idea of your book's 'place' among others.
5. Get in early with an editor – once you've got a target publication date in mind, approach editors to see if they have availability

and book yourself in. It's the same with proofreaders and cover designers.

6. Decide on your publishing route – are you going to try traditional or will you self-publish?
7. Find 3–5 books in your niche/in general non-fiction you'll aim to read over the coming months … and read them!

CHAPTER 5

THE READER'S JOURNEY

When you know who your audience is; who you are writing for; you pass the first hurdle to author success.

Judith Briles

I once met a terrible maths teacher. Sitting with my thirteen-year-old son, Ben, at parents' evening, I was looking forward to hearing about his progress. He always tries really hard, but it's often a struggle. The teacher, however, looked flustered. He shuffled his notes a few times, barely making eye contact with me.

Frankly I was bracing myself for the worst.

Peering across the table at my son, the teacher cleared his throat before uttering three words I never expected to hear.

'Who are you?'

Now, don't get me wrong. I know secondary school teachers see a lot of different children each week, but really? How could he not recognise someone in his maths class? To make matters worse, it wasn't the first time he'd said it. We'd had the same conversation the previous year. I'd given him the benefit of the doubt the first time around, as my son had only been at the school for a term.

But this time – after nearly two years of teaching him – he still didn't know who Ben was.

And his excuse?

'Well, Mrs Caswell, your son must be very well-behaved.' As though that made it okay ...

Writing a book without really knowing your reader is a bit of an insult to them. You need to know where they are on their journey, as well as where they want to be. What they want to get out of the experience. Unlike a teacher, who should know each individual child they teach, you're not able to know each reader by name. But you *are* able to create a picture of them in your mind, which is why it's important you do the ideal reader exercise in the previous chapter.

Sometimes, you're so wrapped up in what *you* want to write about and *your* journey, you almost forget the reader exists. If they're not interested, it must be them that are wrong, not you.

Now I'm pretty confident you're not like that. You're not Ben's maths teacher. But it's easy to slip into writing a book without considering exactly how you're going to take the reader on a journey of transformation and change. You're brimming with ideas and knowledge; you just want to get it down on the page.

And I get that. I really do. But before you write, you have to get a clear idea of your reader and the journey they're on. Not only does it make the book far more helpful for them to read, it also makes it a lot easier for you to write too.

In this chapter, you'll discover how important the reader's journey is and how you can map out a clear route for them to take. It will be full of many journey-related analogies, so, for that, I can only apologise.

Understanding your reader

Your reader must be at the heart of your book. They should be the reason you're writing it. Yes, you want to share your ideas and knowledge to become an expert in your niche, but fundamentally your reader is the most important person.

In the previous chapter, I touched on the idea of giving your reader a name and working out their demographics and psychographics. Doing this makes you feel closer to them and enables you to empathise more easily with their plight. It also helps when the inner critic hops onto your shoulder and makes you consider trying to speak to everyone.

Psychology tells us that people buy with emotion and justify with logic. Our decisions are based on our emotions. So when someone reaches for your book, it's from a place of emotion. Maybe they're hurting or confused. Maybe they're feeling inspired or motivated to change. Tapping into these emotions will make your book stand out.

The reader promise

Consider what promise you're making to your reader. You're not guaranteeing anything, but you're promising tools and strategies for their journey. What they do with them is ultimately up to them.

So what promises will you make to your reader? When sitting down to write this book, I contemplated this very question. And it came down to the following points. I promised to:

- Share all the information I've accumulated over the years on the book-writing process.
- Give you some clarity, so you no longer feel overwhelmed and confused about writing a book.

- Instil confidence in you that you can do this – even if you were shit at writing at school or you're struggling to find time to write.
- Entertain you with my sense of humour – so you smile a little while reading and enjoy the experience.

Now my promises to you may well be different to the promises you make to your reader. I can't guarantee I'll make you smile. You might just think I'm a bit of dick, and I'm okay with that. My voice won't appeal to everyone.

I can't guarantee you'll feel more confident or less overwhelmed either, but I'm going to try my hardest to make sure you do. One thing I can guarantee, however, is that I'll share everything I've learned – I'll feel wrung out like a sponge by the end!

Often, the promises you make to your reader are linked closely to your values. Be they your business values or your personal ones, or a mixture of both. Not only that, making the promises guides you on your writing journey. Once you've completed your book, you can look back and consider whether you've met them. Did you live up to what you said you would? If not, how could you tweak things in the editing process?

The reader's journey

Considering your reader's journey from start to finish is an important part of planning your book. You need to take them by the hand and lead them along the path. Imagine you're walking beside them, holding the lamp aloft to light the way. Let's break this journey down into its component parts.

Base camp

Welcome to your reader's starting point on their journey of learning or transformation. It's at this point they wander into the book shop or surf the internet, looking for a solution.

Your book needs to meet them at this point. It needs to be the answer they're searching for. It needs to be the guide that says, 'I can help.'

As I've mentioned, your reader is at an emotional point here. And it's where your blurb and synopsis are going to do the leg work. Your introduction needs to hook them in, pulling them into your book and promising a solution.

But how?

First and foremost, if you haven't done the exercise from the previous chapter about understanding your ideal reader, go and do that now. Really understanding their emotions and aspirations will help you show empathy and prove you're the guide they need.

The most important question to answer is 'why?' Why are they picking up your book? What's just happened in their life that's spurred them on? Meet them in their current emotional state. Think of the last book you bought, what made you buy it when you did?

The route

Next, consider the journey yourself. Maybe you've already been on it and you're writing from experience. Or maybe you've worked with so many clients who are on a similar journey that you know the similarities. What will your reader need to know and learn as they move ahead? How are you going to get them from base camp to their final destination?

Sometimes this will take on a linear form, where the transformational journey from A to B is fairly straightforward. This book is an example of that. Before you write, you need to get in the right mindset and form good habits. Then you need to understand the planning process, before actually doing the writing. Once you've done that, it's time to think about publication etc.

But other books can be less linear. They just have to follow a path that makes sense. Initially, it'll be in a way that makes sense to you. But before publishing, you'll need to make sure it makes sense to others too.

This is where beta readers come in – something we'll explore later. Essentially, these are the people that will clarify whether you've structured it in a way that makes sense from an outsider's perspective.

Rarely are journeys straightforward, even in real life. So consider the common obstacles or diversions that might crop up for your reader. Does your journey take these into account? If not, how could you build them in as points to discuss?

The final destination

This is where your reader wants to end up. Again, it's important to consider their emotions here. If they started the journey confused, they'll want to have clarity by the end. If they came across your book because they're feeling negative about a certain situation, they'll want to end on a positive note. Emotions really are the key.

Even if you're writing to give someone new knowledge, e.g. about sales funnels or training their dog, you'll still need to consider how this makes them feel emotionally. Feeling confident to take your dog out on a walk without worrying they'll steal food from the nearest picnic blanket is a wonderful feeling. Believe me.

One final thing to consider with the end of the journey is how you want the reader to feel about you as a writer, or as a coach. Or how you want them to feel about your brand. Ideally, they're going to go away and write you a fantastic review and tell all their friends about your book.

So, with that in mind, why not try out this activity?

Put yourself in their shoes. Imagine you've just finished your book. Write a review for it. What would you want it to say? How many stars would you want it to have? What impact did your book have on you? Now print off your review and stick it up. It'll work nicely to motivate you and remind you of what you're striving for.

Struggling to understand your reader?

If you're not completely sure of your reader's pain points or challenges, there are plenty of places to find them. Here are a few options to try:

- Ask your audience – use social media or your email list to your advantage. Tell them you're writing a book and you'd love their help. If any of their responses are really interesting, you could use them as case studies further down the line.
- Use your competitors – look at their social media. What's coming up in the comments? How are people reacting? What questions are they asking?
- Check out Amazon/Goodreads reviews – as mentioned in the previous chapter, these can be a gold mine for things people are wanting to know but haven't found yet. You can also see what people really enjoyed in the 5* reviews.
- Look on forums – what are the questions people are asking? What advice are they seeking? These can help further down the planning process too.

Set a timer for this sort of thing. Otherwise you'll end up spending too long on it and eventually you'll get a case of 'comparisonitis'. This is research only. Don't get sucked in.

Summary

Understanding your reader means putting yourself in their place. Immersing yourself in their world. Meeting them where they're at. For some of you, you'll be writing from real experience. You'll show them the empathy that comes from walking a mile in their shoes. Even if you haven't clocked up the blisters yourself, you'll need to speak to them as though you have.

The best books I've ever read speak to me directly. If I read Brené Brown, I know I'm guaranteed to feel various emotions. Often I feel seen but also understood like never before. If I read Jen Sincero, I know I'm going to get a kick up the butt while laughing at the same time. I'll be in different emotional places when I reach for them too. I look for Brené's reassuring words when I need a comforting ear. I'll reach for Jen when I know I need a boot up the bum to get out of a slump.

Your reader will feel the same about your work. It's worth repeating; people buy with emotions and justify with logic. So which emotions are your readers feeling when they reach for your book?

Action steps

1. Create your ideal reader avatar (if you haven't already) – use the questions in the previous chapter to help you.
2. Focus on your reader's psychographics – emotions fuel purchases, so get to grips with where they're at.
3. Look at reviews on Amazon or Goodreads – what do people want? What have the other books failed to give them?
4. Do some research on social media – look for recurring emotional words your ideal reader is using. You can either use these in your book, in your marketing strategy or just for information.
5. Consider each phase of your reader's journey – from base camp to final destination. What are the obstacles that typically come up on their journey – use your own experience or that of your clients.
6. Find a school where the staff know your child's name.

CHAPTER 6

BIG-PICTURE PLANNING

"Phoebe, do you have a plan?"
"I don't even have a pla ..."
Phoebe Buffay and Monica Geller

Moving house is one of the most stressful things you can do. It's fraught with timelines, disappointments, excitement and solicitors who drag the process out more than should be legally allowed.

When you start looking for a new house, there's plenty to consider: location, budget and quality of the nearest schools ... whether it has a nearby Lidl. Each person's preferences and desires are different. How people manage this process is different too. For some, it will involve spreadsheets and lists. For others, it will involve nothing more than turning up to a viewing and getting a feel for the place.

For most people though, buying a house means being part of a chain. Whether big or small, breaks in the chain can have a catastrophic effect on the process. Taking it from excitement to devastation in one foul phone call. Unless you know the house you're moving into is ready and available, you're not going anywhere.

Or are you?

My friend Nancy isn't a planner. She's not someone who takes big decisions too seriously. She's more of a 'let's see where things take us' type of gal. Essentially, the opposite of me. If I'm going on holiday, I'll have everything printed off and put into plastic wallets. If Nancy turned up to the airport without her passport, she'd just laugh and see it as all part of the adventure.

The same can be said for her house-buying process. Recently, Nancy bought a new house. A gorgeous property that was everything she wanted and more. The trouble was, there had been a hold-up in the part of the chain above them. Not wishing to lose their buyer, Nancy decided to take a rather unique plan of action. Putting everything into storage, they sold their flat and took the opportunity to go on holiday, assuming the new house would be ready when they got back in two weeks' time.

Assuming.

If it wasn't? Well, they'd cross that bridge when they came to it.

When she told me this, I broke out into a cold sweat. Her plan of action filled me with dread. I couldn't imagine going on holiday with the possibility I'd be homeless when I returned, especially since they had a six-month-old baby in tow. I couldn't just cross my fingers and hope for the best. I'd be in the corner of a room in the foetal position, sipping gin through a straw.

But Nancy? Nancy was so laid back she was almost horizontal.

And that's the point. How I'd plan for a big move is not the same as Nancy would. Planning for things is very individual. What one person might do is very different from another.

And it's the same for writing.

Planning your book's content

Now you've got your umbrella plan in place, it's time to turn your attention to the content of your book. Big-picture planning is where you take everything you know about your topic and start putting it onto paper. You might have already done this to some extent, but this process will not only get your thoughts out of your head; it will get them into some sense of order.

Often when people try to write a book, they sit down without a plan and just write. Normally, this only gets them so far. In the world of fiction writing, these authors are affectionately known as 'pantsers' – flying into the writing process by the seat of their pants, letting their characters lead the way. Those who plan meticulously are called 'plotters' – they know every detail about every chapter. Surprises are rare.

I like to sit somewhere in the middle. Maybe that makes me a 'plantser', who knows? With non-fiction writing, having a more detailed outline can be more helpful and give your book a better structure. But don't be surprised if, when you're writing your first draft, you include things you haven't planned for. It's just creativity at play.

Your big-picture plan and your outline (which we'll cover in the next chapter) are here to take the overwhelm away. How much you plan is entirely up to you – it's a personal preference. Hopefully these two chapters will give you the clarity and the confidence to start … and continue.

Oh, and Nancy? She arrived back from holiday and moved straight into her new home. Turns out, being laid back pays off.

Big-picture planning

If you're anything like me, you'll have had a book idea swirling around in your head for a while, months or even years. It's time to empty your head of all your ideas. I like to think they've been percolating like a fine wine, ready to be decanted onto the page.

How you do this bit of the planning stage is up to you. I've used spider diagrams in notebooks, lists on pieces of flipchart paper and, most recently, a board on Trello – an online collaboration tool that allows you to organise your projects digitally. I'm a very visual learner, so these types of things work well for me. You need to use whatever works for you.

There are four stages to this process, so let's look at them in more detail.

Step 1: The brain dump

Does exactly what it says on the tin. It's an opportunity for you to take all your ideas and dump them down onto paper/Trello board. Just go with the flow.

- Set a timer for 15–20 minutes – an intense block of time to get your thoughts down.
- Find a space where you won't be disturbed and turn off any distractions.
- Fire up your Trello board or grab your piece of paper and a pen.
- Start your timer and, in that period of time, write down everything you can possibly think of about your book's content.
- Whatever you do, don't try to justify or second guess your choices. Just let them flow out. The time to sort them comes later.
- Keep writing and writing until the timer goes. You'll be surprised at the gems you unearth when you really dig deep.

When the timer goes, sit back and relax. It's an intense process, but also an immensely satisfying one. Leave your list/board/spider diagram to one side for the moment. Over the next few days, you'll begin to think of other ideas to add. It'll be when you're doing the most unlikely tasks, e.g. taking a shower, walking the dog, plucking your eyebrows.

In the world of neuroscience it's called 'spontaneous and cognitive creativity' – first classified by psychiatrist Arne Dietrich in 2004. Once you've got the predictable ideas down on paper using your prefrontal cortex, your basal ganglia take over. While you're working on something else like watering the plants or brushing your teeth, your subconscious is still busy thinking about ideas. Free from the constraints of consciousness, the basal ganglia play around with the information and produce new ideas. It's why we feel like we're having 'lightbulb' moments – they seem so effortless and spontaneous.

This is one of the reasons I've started using Trello, as I can add to my board by using the app on my phone when I'm out and about.

Keep adding to your list of ideas for the next few days. You'll keep adding to it as you outline and write your first draft. Your brain won't be creative at a time that suits you. So keep your notebook handy and transfer your ideas as they come to you. Again, don't analyse them. Just jot them down. Some will never get used and that's fine. This isn't the time to worry about that.

Step 2: Organisation into groups

You've got all these brilliant ideas, but they're a little haphazard. As you've been dumping these ideas down, you've probably realised you're able to see common themes between them. Ways in which you can group some of these ideas together. This is the starting point for your chapter headings.

If you've done your brain dump on a sheet of paper, it's time to make things pretty. Grab a few different coloured pens or highlighters. Using one colour, start to highlight or circle ideas that could be grouped together under one common topic. Once you've found all the ideas that fit together, choose another colour and repeat the process.

Keep going until you've grouped all your ideas in groups of colours. Don't worry about what these groups are going to be called yet. If you've got some that don't fit into any group, don't panic. We'll come onto those in a minute.

If you're using Trello, start creating lists of ideas – grouping common ones together in one list and then creating another list for the next group. If you want more support with using Trello for this stage of Big-Picture Planning, head on over to my website and watch the video at creatinghappywriters.com/daretowrite.

Stage 3: Group headings

Things are slowly beginning to take shape now. You're able to see ideas that come under a common theme. If you're not using Trello, you'll need another sheet of paper. You might even want to consider using a spreadsheet which, to be fair, is just a simpler version of Trello.

You'll need to create lists/columns now. Each column represents one of the colours you've used to highlight/circle. On your sheet of paper, write down everything under one colour in one list. Then repeat for all the other colours. So you've now got lists of common ideas.

If you've been using Trello all along, you'll have done this when creating your board.

Now is the time to look at each list. What might be a good title for that particular list? What umbrella name could all the ideas be grouped under? These titles are going to become your working chapter headings. Note the word 'working' – nothing is set in stone at this stage; it's just initial planning.

Go to each list in turn and think of a name for it. If you're using Trello, make this the title of each list. If you're on paper, write down the potential chapter heading at the top of each column.

Now things are looking a bit tasty. Your chapters are developing in front of your very eyes and a structure begins to take shape.

But what about those pesky ideas that didn't fit under any category/in any list? Look at them again. Can they go anywhere now you've begun sorting your ideas? If not, are they big enough to be chapters on their own?

If not, it's time to get brutally honest. Either leave them to one side to look at again once you're outlining. Or, if you're brave, strike them off altogether. In the literary world, you'd call this 'killing your darlings'. In my world, we'll just call it 'killing off stuff that doesn't fit'. Trusting your gut instinct often works well at this stage. And remember, it's not as though you can't add them in at another time during the writing process.

Maybe I should call it 'killing off stuff that doesn't fit … for now'?

Stage 4: Editing the list

Look at the Trello board/lists you've created. It's time to get out the metaphorical red pen … or the real one, if that works.

From now on we're going to call these lists your 'chapters' because this is a book about writing, not shopping. Take one chapter at a time and ask yourself these questions:

- Is this essential to the chapter?
- Is this idea under the best chapter heading? Does it need to move to another?
- Have I repeated this idea in another way in any other part of this chapter?

- Do I want to include this idea?
- Does it contribute to the reader's journey? How?

If there's anything that doesn't cut the mustard, cross it out/delete it from your board. If you're not sure yet, leave it for now and when you're writing your draft, you may find that it doesn't quite fit where you expected it to or doesn't fit at all.

Other things to consider

During this phase of the planning process, there are also a few other things that you'll need to consider.

Your book title

You might have an idea for a book title already, but I would urge you to keep it as a 'working title' for the time being. Once you've written the book, you'll be able to look back and decide whether it's still the right choice. Try not to get bogged down with this decision; it really is just an idea at the moment. You'll have plenty of other opportunities to work on it.

One thing to consider is that you'll need to use a title that's 'search engine friendly', particularly if you're self-publishing on Amazon. If your book is about career change, you'll need to keep that in the title somewhere, even if it's in the tagline underneath. You need to make it as easy as possible for potential readers to find it.

Your introduction

It's often daunting to write the very first word on the very first page of your book. In non-fiction, this is almost always the introduction. You stare at the blinking cursor and wonder what on earth you should write. It's often the stumbling block for many.

Well here's how to make it easier. Write the introduction last. Plan for it last too. How on earth are you supposed to know what you're introducing if you haven't written it yet? The same can be said for the small introductions to each chapter. Plan for each one once you've planned out the rest of the chapter.

Introductions are used to show empathy and understanding for your reader. In your main introduction, you'll need to plan to meet the reader where they're at. You'll need to show you understand exactly what it's like to be feeling how they're feeling. You might do this from personal experience or from other stories to show your understanding.

Storytelling and anecdotes

Stories have been part of the fabric of society for thousands of years. Our brains are wired to tell stories and to listen to them. Nonfiction books need stories to make them entertaining to read. Some of the best books I've read have stories at the heart of them.

In *The Obstacle is the Way* by Ryan Holiday, he uses stories to hook you throughout your reading experience, telling tales of the stoics. In *You Are a Badass at Making Money* by Jen Sincero, she sprinkles stories throughout to keep you smiling. If you're familiar with Jen's work, you'll know the one about the goats breaking into the house she was staying in … Still cracks me up just thinking about it.

But it's not just stories for entertainment's sake. It's because it gives you, the writer, an opportunity to share a story that puts the reader at the heart of the adventure. Your reader becomes the hero. And yes, while Jen's goat story is about an experience she had personally, you can relate to being in similar sticky situations and it's relevant to the chapter.

One word of warning with using stories and anecdotes, though. Often, as authors, we're keen to share our experiences. We hope people will learn from mistakes we've made or lessons we've learned. But don't saturate your book with them. I like to think of stories as the seasoning in a recipe. You wouldn't overload your favourite pasta dish with salt, would you? Same needs to be said for stories in non-fiction.

Use them to highlight how the reader is feeling or to briefly illustrate a point, but then move on.

During the planning stage, simply jot down the story you wish to use. In Jen's case, she may have written 'goat story' in her planning process. Don't soak up important planning time with details, just get the general story idea down and move on.

Research

The amount of research you need for your book will vary, depending on your existing knowledge and also the tone of your book. Some authors like to share statistics to back up points they're making. Others like to cite further research that readers can go away and read.

There's no hard and fast rule. During the planning process, you may be tempted to spend a lot of time in the research phase. It's important to be accurate, but it's also important to actually start writing. Often, research is procrastination in one of its many disguises. We tell ourselves we need to do a little bit more of it before we'll feel ready to write. The truth is, I'm not sure you'll ever feel 'ready' to write. It's one of those things you just have to crack on with.

What I tend to do in the big-picture planning phase is simply write down the research I need to do. It might be a quote or it might be a case study. But I don't spend time worrying about the precise content of it now. I just put down a reminder card on Trello or in my notebook, so that when it comes to outlining and writing the first draft, I'm aware of what needs to be done.

I urge you to do the same.

Contributors and professionals

During this initial planning phase, put some thought into who else needs to come on board this book journey with you.

Contributors are often people who are experts in their field. You know you'd love them to write a chapter or a few pages for your book, to add greater depth to your work. Now's the time to approach them with exactly what you'd like them to do. Avoid being too wishy-washy with your request. Be clear with your brief. Most people will feel flattered that you've asked them. Being clear with a deadline is really helpful too.

Now is also the time to think about editors, cover designers and proofreaders. These professionals will help your book be the best it can be. But don't underestimate how busy they are.

My advice is to approach an editor before you've written your first draft. Why? Firstly, to book in their time. But also because it's a wonderful accountability exercise too. If you've told your editor you're going to get your book to them on a certain date, it really can be the kick up the bum you need.

We'll cover all the professionals you'll need to consider in Chapter 10.

Summary

You're ready to begin your big-picture plan! You'll feel a sense of real excitement as you piece together the first stages of your book's structure. Do remember this is just an initial plan. It's likely chapters will move around and change once you begin outlining and writing. Avoid spending hours fretting over this big-picture plan. Instead, simply get all your ideas down and put them into what seems like a logical order.

If you can, set aside a whole day for this activity. It's more likely to get done if you prioritise it in this way. It's also hugely satisfying to take a big leap towards your outline in just a few hours. It can be mentally draining though, so be prepared to feel creatively exhausted by the end. As previously mentioned, do give your umbrella plan a few days to percolate and improve.

Your prefrontal cortex does the initial hard work, but it's the basal ganglia that are the real winners here, helping you think of further additions to your plan long after you've shut your laptop or stepped away from your notebook. Keep adding to your plan but avoid looking for 'perfection' – again, another form of procrastination. As soon as it's looking in pretty good shape, it's time to move on to the outline.

Action steps

1. Complete the 5 W planning activities – it will really help you get a clear picture of your book and inspire you to get outlining. In order to get where you want to go, you need to know where you're coming from. For further support on this stage of the planning process, do watch the masterclass video on my website - creatinghappywriters.com/daretowrite.
2. Make a list of any contributors and professionals you'll need to approach – send out some emails to give people enough time to prepare their part or book you a slot in their calendar.
3. When you've created your plan, look at which stories might fit into each chapter. Only do this by jotting down the story concept in a sentence or two – you'll be able to flesh it out properly later.
4. Use Trello or paper to complete your lists – consider initial chapter headings for each list. These can change but it's a good idea to have an initial idea. You'll find some come more easily than others. Struggling to think of an appropriate heading? Leave it and come back to it later.
5. When moving house, be more Nancy.

CHAPTER 7

OUTLINING YOUR BOOK

The outline is 95 percent of the book. Then I sit down and write, and that's the easy part.

Jeffery Deaver

I'm a big fan of the TV show *Grand Designs* – maybe I'm secretly harbouring a desire to build my own home, who knows? One of the things I love about it is the journey people go on when taking on a self-build project. Not only does the presenter, Kevin McCloud, delight in people's initial enthusiasm, he's positively gleeful when they give him their suggested completion date.

You see, self-builders often have a rose-tinted view of the coming months. No matter what Kevin says, they're convinced they'll stay on budget and complete their new house in the time they've allocated. Even when he raises his eyebrows and delivers a wry smile, they won't be put off. Not even when his eyes bulge out of their sockets when one of them claims they'll be project manager too, while holding down a full-time job.

Fast forward to several months or even years later, and it's a different story. Kevin sits in their beautiful new home and asks the question, 'So how much did you spend in the end?' Cue nervous giggles and shakes of the head as couples sheepishly admit they've gone over budget and it's taken them far longer than they ever imagined.

Yet despite all the setbacks they've had, almost every couple is thrilled with the outcome. It's the house they've dreamed of. They couldn't be happier. And the reason? A clear plan. Almost all of them have architects' drawings to work from. And while they may have changed things along the way, success happens by following this to the letter.

It's the same for your book. The equivalent to an architect's plan is your outline. Something you can follow to ensure you're happy with the outcome of your book. Instead of a house you've always dreamed of owning, it's a book you've always dreamed of writing.

Now you may be recoiling slightly at the mere mention of an outline. If that's you, can I politely ask you to reconsider? Particularly if you've tried writing before and given up, declaring that it simply isn't for you. An outline isn't meant to constrain your creativity. Rather, it's meant to cocoon it in a gentle way, stopping you from veering off course and feeling overwhelmed.

If, however, you really can't be persuaded to outline in the way I'm about to describe, read on anyway. See it as something you can actively rebel against – sticking two fingers up at me as you sail off into the writing distance. No hard feelings.

But, if like a large percentage of the population, you're someone who needs a strategy and an outline to follow, you're in for a treat. Outlining is often the step that enables you to really gain the confidence to complete your first draft. It adds detail to the umbrella plan you've already started.

Going back to the marathon analogy in Chapter 1, it's the detail of every training run, so you know how far to run and for how long. In writing terms, it means putting in the details of each chapter, so you know exactly what to write and when, during your first draft.

If you've never written a book before, your outline makes all the difference, not only in ensuring you include the most pertinent details, but also in giving you a huge dose of confidence. You'll head into the shitty first draft feeling like a champion.

Now, I'm sharing with you an outlining process that has worked for me. It has enabled me to write six books in just over six years. Without it, my first book would have stayed as an idea in my head. This very book would have been harder to write. But, as with anything, you can take from it what works for you. If you want to follow it to the letter, great. If you want to dip in and out of this model, you can do that too.

Let's dive in.

Step 1: Subheadings

You're about to make a new best friend. Say hello to subheadings, your travelling companion who will signpost your writing into a logical sequence. But why do we need to use them? Well, it gives your reader a chance to have a mini break from reading. It helps their brain to compartmentalise what it's read and brings a section of writing to a satisfying conclusion.

You've probably read books with reams of writing and they're hard to digest. You want your reader to have a satisfying experience and subheadings can contribute to this.

At the moment, you've got your lists on either a Trello board or a sheet of paper. Each list has a chapter heading, taking your reader on their journey from start to finish. Now it's time to look at each list in turn.

Take your first list and look at all the content you've brain dumped into it. Now break this list down into sections. Some of your ideas will be big enough to be sections on their own. Some may be smaller, so see whether any of those ideas could logically be grouped together into a section under a common title.

Each section is going to need a subheading. Sometimes these subheadings can be one word – like in this section you're reading. Or you can use questions to create subheadings too – this is often a useful method. Why? Because you can use a commonly asked question and then answer it in the section underneath. I tend to use a mixture of both.

Here's an example to help you. Ironically, this section of this book about subheadings needed a subheading ... called subheadings. Phew! Try saying that after a gin or two. My umbrella plan had quite a few ideas for this section, including using questioning and breaking down your ideas. I knew it would be a large enough section to stand alone with its own subheading.

However, in a previous chapter you'll have noticed I've used a subheading called 'Other things to consider'. This is where I'd grouped smaller ideas together that wouldn't necessarily be individual sections on their own. So I scooped them up under one subheading that would encompass them all.

Now it's your turn. Take a look at your first list and start developing your subheadings. Repeat the process for each of your chapter lists, finding the subheadings that make sense to you. Again, these can be changed during the writing/editing process, but just go with what feels right for now.

Step 2: Expanding your sections

Now you've got your subheadings sorted, it's time to open up a document that will become your shitty first draft. Exciting! You might want to investigate Scrivener, software created specifically for writers. I use Google Docs, so I can access my manuscript wherever I am. You'll need either your Trello board on hand or your notebook beside you.

Open up your document. I tend to write my first draft as one document, rather than having separate ones for each chapter, but the choice is obviously yours. Your first page will be your introduction, but as you're not writing that until the end, you can simply type 'Introduction' and then add in a section break to start a new page.

Take your first list and your first chapter heading. Type that at the top of the page. Then look at your subheadings. Write each subheading on the page until they look like a list.

Now go to the first subheading and create some bullet points under it of things you know you're going to include in that section. These might be ideas from your plan or just points you know from your knowledge and expertise. Include as many bullet points as you need under that first subheading and then move onto the next one.

You're beginning to fill out your chapters in note form. Simply jotting your ideas down into the document like this helps you to see your first draft taking shape. Here's an example of a section I outlined for *Keeping Bums in Seats*, in the chapter entitled 'Working with Parents':

How can you build good communication with parents? (SUBHEADING)

- Flexibility with communication channels
- Be proactive
- Approachability and availability
- Discretion
- Apologise if you make a mistake

And that was it! Just a few bullet points that could then be turned into paragraphs/full sentences during the first draft. It really doesn't need to be any more detailed than that.

Step 3: Adding in any extras

Now's the time to look at each of your outlined chapters and add in anything else you want to include, such as:

- Case studies
- Contributor sections
- Anecdotes/personal stories
- Research that needs to be done

Remember not to get bogged down in the details here. Keep it simple. Just jot down what needs to happen and move on. Imagine these as notes for your future self. Only use case studies/anecdotes that are helpful to the reader. If they don't add anything to the reader's experience, leave them out.

Step 4: Summaries and action steps

You might want to include these two features in your book: summaries and action steps. They're not essential and may not be relevant for your book, but they're worth considering. So what are they and how can they help your book's structure?

Summaries

At the end of longer chapters, it's useful to have a summary for the reader. Essentially, it's a quick overview of what they've just read, including the most pertinent bits that are worth repeating. It can help bring the chapter to a close in a nice way too. It also enables you to prepare the reader for what's coming next.

Action steps

Readers love to take action. Action steps are quick strategies they can take away from the experience and try out in real life. Again, this might not be relevant for your book, but I use the action steps in books as journalling prompts to get me thinking in a different way. Often, they'll help me make progress towards a goal I have (often the reason I picked up the book), but sometimes it's just a great reflection tool.

Stage 5: Head back to the chapter introduction

Finally, it's time to consider the introduction to each chapter. Once you've done the outline for it, head back to the start of the chapter and think about what you might want to include in the introduction. A good place to start is establishing why that chapter is important to the reader and managing their expectations.

Let them know what's going to feature in this chapter and what they can hope to learn. If you're still stuck with this bit, leave it. Come back to introductions when the rest of your first draft is complete.

Once you've completed the entire book's outline, you can consider the introduction to the *whole* book. You'll know what you're introducing now! Often, these sections feature in the introduction to any non-fiction book:

- A story to hook your reader – often personal. It's linked to the reason you're writing the book and shows empathy too.
- A section to show you understand where they're at emotionally – it's a great place to get direct with them and tell them you know what it's like. You understand how they're feeling.
- Your reader promise – let them know what you're hoping they'll get out of reading your book. How you want them to feel at the end.
- Manage their expectations – if it's going to be a difficult journey, acknowledge that and put their mind at rest.
- A 'how to read this book' – quite often people like to know if they should read the whole thing from start to finish or whether they can dip in and out of sections that are more pertinent. It's

also a great place to mention action steps/case studies and why you've included them.

A good way to consider the introduction to your book is to imagine you're introducing it as a talk or speech. What would you say then? What would you want the reader to know or understand at this point?

One more thing ...

You may be struggling to consider doing this much writing at this point. Not everyone is a writer. Not everyone enjoys the process. So why not consider dictating your ideas?

If you find it easier to say your plans out loud, dictation can work really well in the planning stages. Not only that, Microsoft Word has a 'dictate' function to help you. All you do is speak into your computer's microphone and it transcribes what you're saying.

Summary

Outlining your book takes the pressure off writing your first draft. As mentioned in Chapter 3 on habits and productivity, it's getting things moving which is the first hurdle. Outlining does that for you. It's the force that pushes past inertia so momentum kicks in.

It also gives you confidence. Your book takes shape before your eyes and you finally get that little burst of excitement as your ideas flow. No, it's not always easy. But it's so much better than trying to make it up as you go along. You'll only get so far if you try that, particularly if it's your first book.

Take it one chapter at a time. One subheading at a time. One bullet point at a time. And sooner or later your outline is complete and you're fully prepared to tackle the shitty first draft.

Action steps

1. Outline the chapters in your book – if you're not sure about a particular section yet, just leave it and come back to it. Give your brain a chance to ponder the content and you might just be surprised at how quickly you're able to fill in the gaps.
2. Use questions for some of your subheadings – consider what question your reader might be asking at different stages. This can really help structure your sections, as you simply need to give a detailed answer.
3. Begin noting down possible action steps for your reader – what would move them along their journey to transformation or new knowledge? The irony of writing an action step about action steps isn't lost on me, I can assure you ...
4. Consider case studies or examples you could use to back up the points you're making. These aren't essential, but sometimes they help explain a point in more detail.
5. Are there particular quotes you'd want to use in each chapter to motivate your reader? These could be famous ones or comments your clients have made in the past.
6. Avoid getting bogged down into too much detail – keep it brief. You'll have the shitty first draft to flesh out your ideas further.
7. If you apply for Grand Designs, hire a project manager - Kevin will then have nothing to gloat about.

CHAPTER 8

WRITING YOUR FIRST DRAFT

(AKA THE SFD)

"On the field of The Self stand a knight and a dragon.
You are the knight. Resistance is the dragon."
Steven Pressfield

When dealing with a toddler, you experience many battles. Yes, with your own sanity, but also with the wilfulness of a small, determined human. My youngest son, Beau, was quite the single-minded tot. He did things in his own time, at his own pace, including learning to walk. He quite enjoyed being carried around, thank you very much. Walk? When he could be carried like a king? Absolutely not. Walking was for peasants.

He had a similar attitude to toilet training. He wasn't going to use a potty if it got in the way of more exciting things like playing with his cars or watching *Mickey Mouse Clubhouse*. Particularly if it was a No.

2. No siree. Using his pants was a far more appealing option. One evening, he and big-brother Ben were playing on the bunk beds when Ben called out:

'Code Brown!'

I rushed upstairs to find a lovely parcel of poo on Ben's pillow. Exasperated, I turned to Beau and said:

'Why did you do a poo in Ben's bed?'

Giving me a look of incredulity, he simply shrugged and replied:

'Well, at least it wasn't in my pants, Mummy!'

Now, you may be wondering what Beau's toilet training has to do with you writing a book. As much as I'd love to say it's because I call the first draft 'the shitty first draft', it's more about the battle you've got ahead of you. Much like the battle I had with Beau to get him to walk and toilet like a regular person.

Because this is the point in the process where you need to be prepared for battle ... with yourself. Now that might sound a little harsh, but this part of the process often tests writers – both new and experienced. You're battling between analytical mode and creative mode. You're battling your inner critic. You're battling against time.

In order to step onto the battlefield fully prepared, you'll need some armour. The good thing is, you're already wearing it. All the chapters preceding this have prepared you for the fight ahead. It's why I wrote this book in the way I did. You've got to make friends with your inner critic. You've got to establish good habits. You've got to have a plan. All of these pull together now, to help you with what lies ahead.

You'll have days ahead where you won't want to open your laptop. If that happens, I can only recommend you give yourself a day away from it. Give your brain a break from the constant demand. But once you've had a day or two away, get back into it, otherwise days turn into weeks.

Your book goes back to being an idea you once had and never sees the light of day.

So grab your armour and let's go.

Making friends with the shitty first draft

Author Terry Pratchett once said, 'The first draft is just you telling yourself the story.' Now, while you're not writing a novel, this is also true for writing non-fiction. Your first draft is you getting to know your book. Imagine it's someone you've just met and been introduced to. You know a little bit about them (your outline), but now you've got time to sit down and really get to know them.

You won't necessarily like all they have to say during your encounters, but gradually you'll grow attached to them. You'll look forward to your daily time together. Remind yourself, this is a process. You're not going to wake up tomorrow and miraculously be an author. If only ...

It's worth remembering that no one else will see this first draft. No one. Not your editor, not your beta readers, not even your friends. So as you're writing, remind yourself you'll get to polish your work before anyone gets to see it. Books you see in the shops aren't first drafts. They've been through so many revisions; they will be nothing like the authors' first attempts. Don't compare your first draft to their tenth. It's incomparable.

How to go from your outline to your first draft

Your outline means you'll never face a blank page. You'll never sit down and not know what to write. That's why I recommend you create one. But now you have this wonderful outline, what do you do with it?

Your bullet points take centre stage. Working hard for you and giving you a basic structure. For each chapter, you'll need to go to each section and flesh out each bullet. Depending on the point you're making, this will either be a paragraph or a couple of sentences.

Take the bullet point and just write. Imagine you're saying this out loud if it helps. If you were explaining this point verbally, what would you say? Quite often, I speak the sentences as I'm typing. Especially if it's something a bit more complex. It also helps you check to see if it sounds right. Remember to write your introductions last too.

Writing and editing

But a word of caution here. Avoid deleting and rewriting sentences. It stops the flow. Positive psychologist Mihály Csíkszentmihályi described flow as 'a state of complete immersion in an activity'. You're in the zone. It's what you're aiming for – stopping and starting makes the process harder.

As you type, remind yourself you'll come back and edit at a later time. Have a mantra if it helps. But whatever you do, resist the urge to edit and write at the same time.

I want you to imagine you have two sides of the writing brain. One side is creative; the other is analytical.

When writing your book, you must work in either one or the other. Never both at the same time. It was a mistake I made when writing my first book. I'd write a paragraph, reread it and try to make changes. It was hopeless. I never got very far in a writing session and I almost gave up.

It was only when I read about the habits of another writer that things began to change. She avoided reading anything back until she'd completely finished the first draft. Each day, she would read the last sentence of the previous paragraph and just continue on.

It is something I've done ever since. And it's served me well. In fact, at this stage of my first SFD, I've written 19,479 words and I've not read any of them back yet.

You see, your shitty first draft requires you to be in creative mode. And *only* in creative mode. You may be tempted (actually, you *will* be tempted) to go back and look at your work. I still am and this is my sixth book. But whatever you do, don't give in to the urge. The time will come when you'll go into full analytical mode until your heart's content.

Research reminder

It's natural to feel the need to do your research as you go. You might come to a section and feel a bit lost as you haven't got the notes you need to fill in the content completely.

Try not to get sucked into research at this point. Get the main body of the book completed and then go back to research what you need. Stopping to complete research also breaks your flow. Moreover, by writing a large percentage of the book, you'll be a lot clearer on what it is you need to research.

It stops countless hours of research you may never end up using. You may think you need the research to write your book, but if you're ready to write a book, it's likely you've got the knowledge you need already – at least enough to write the first draft. Any additional research will only enhance it in later drafts.

Habits reminder

It's at this point your habit practice will really come into fruition. Planning and outlining is hard, yes, but it's over quite quickly. Writing your first draft is where you're in for the long haul. You'll need to turn up consistently and do the work.

If you haven't established habits to make this process less challenging, go back to the habits chapter and work out what yours will be. Set your word-count target too. You'll then develop the consistency you'll need to get from start to finish.

Let your accountability partner know you're about to start your SFD too. It's a great way to kickstart the process. Announce it on social media if you're so inclined. You'd be amazed at how supportive people are and how much they'll enjoy cheering you along. Little bursts of encouragement can do the world of good.

If you bring your audience along, they're far more likely to buy your book when it's published. You've got ready-made readers right there, so you may as well tap into that while you can.

Summary

You may have expected the chapter about actually writing your book to be longer. But it's time to just crack on and write. Now you know what to expect and how to do it, it really is down to you. If it helps, imagine me sitting beside you and giving you words of encouragement – I'll keep the sarcasm to a minimum, I promise.

Be prepared for a slump too. When you first start out, you're motivated and excited about what lies ahead. As you approach the end, the finish line is in sight and you're striving to reach it.

But the middle? The middle is a bit ... boggy. In fiction writing, we call it 'the soggy middle'. For non-fiction writing, I'll rename it 'the boggy middle'. It's where you're in deep, wading through your content and wondering if you'll drown in the process. At this point, you might need further incentives.

If you haven't been logging your word count, why not start? It may give you the motivation you need. Check in with your accountability partner or writing coach on a regular basis. Whatever you do, don't let the boggy middle defeat you. You'll keep wading through until, eventually, you'll find solid ground. The end is on the horizon and you'll feel a sudden surge of excitement, pushing you closer.

At all times, keep your outline close by. Refer back to it each time you've done a section of your chapter so you don't veer off course. It's a handy reminder of what you're going to include. You'll be grateful you took the time to complete it.

I really wish you luck with the SFD. I'm also excited for you because I know how good it feels to finish. It's such a rush and one that will stick with you for years to come.

Now just get on with it and I'll see you on the other side.

Action steps

1. Keep your outline nearby and start your first draft – it's going to be shitty, but that's okay. You're prepared for it, so knock 'em dead. Flesh out those bullet points and watch the SFD evolve before your eyes.
2. Finalise your daily word count and get your habits in place – where and when will you write? What time of day works best for you?
3. Let your accountability partner know you're starting and set up how often you'll log your word count with them. Establish when it's okay to contact them and how often.
4. Don't give up.
5. Write.
6. When dealing with a stubborn toddler who is refusing to be toilet-trained, it's perfectly acceptable to question your decision to procreate.

CHAPTER 9

EDITING

The secret to editing your work is simple: you need to become its reader instead of its writer.

Zadie Smith

One of the delights of deputy headship was working alongside a wonderful headteacher called Sarah.

Working together closely gave us plenty of opportunities to learn a lot about each other. Sarah loves midget gems, for example. I know exactly how she drinks her tea. She likes nothing more than celebrating the weekend with a pint of Guinness and plenty of sport on the box.

For all the years we worked together, Sarah had a cleaner. One of my favourite things about this was that Sarah or her husband would always clean the house before the cleaner arrived. It always made me smile because it showed the kind of person Sarah is – kind, considerate and generous.

It also reminds me about the editing process. Yes, you're getting a professional editor on board, but you still need to do a bit of editing first. You're going to be Sarah. Cleaning the loo before the cleaner comes ... to also clean the loo. You're being considerate of your editor. Sending them a manuscript that's in the best shape you can make it.

But first you've going to mould it into shape. Editing is where the magic happens. It's where you take something in its roughest form and chip away at it until you've got your (midget) gem.

An editor won't take on a first draft. If you do try to send one to them, they're likely to send it back and suggest you do a round of edits first. It's just too big a job. But not only that, self-editing is an important part of the process for you as a writer. It allows you to 'tinker under the bonnet' and start to make improvements before you let anyone else look at it.

If you're anything like me, you wouldn't dream of letting your neighbour's dog read your first draft, never mind a professional editor. You'll save yourself time, but you'll also see how much your book can grow and change with just your watchful eye.

So I can only strongly urge you to begin the editing process yourself. Don't worry about your grammar and punctuation skills. Don't worry if you're unsure where to begin. We'll cover it all in this chapter, giving you the confidence to send your manuscript to your beta readers and then onto your editor.

Before you begin

Take some time away from your manuscript. As long as you can bear it, but the minimum should be a week, preferably two. You need to give each other some space – similar to the space required from your in-laws after Christmas. Step away completely and give your brain a rest. You'll come back to it with fresh eyes, and editing will be far easier.

Secondly, get ready for the next phase of your journey. As I explained in the previous chapter, editing engages a very different part of your brain to writing. Yes, you'll need some creativity, but it's really the time when your analytical skills come into play. Taking a step back from your manuscript severs the emotional tie you might feel. You've done a great job, but now you need to make it even better.

Finally, I thoroughly recommend you print your book out. Editing is much easier on paper. It's easier to view it in a different medium – if all you've done is look at it on a screen, it can help give you a different perspective. If, however, you don't wish to waste paper, try using a different font while you're editing, as this can help too.

As you move through editing, complete each phase and make changes, before moving onto the next. Try to see your first draft as a working document, something that's constantly evolving and changing as you go through the process.

And back up the bloomin' thing, please. There's nothing quite so horrible as losing your work. Be it the first draft or the tenth, it's like a punch in the gut. So save your work in more than one place so if the worst should happen, you're covered.

Stage 1: Read the whole book

Avoid diving into editing the first draft without reading through the whole book first. You need to know what you're working with. Don't worry if you notice spelling mistakes or things that don't make sense. You'll come back to that. Just read it. See how it flows. Get a feel for what you've produced. Consider how you feel about it as a first attempt.

I tend to keep a notebook beside me during this part of the process. Mainly to avoid changing things as I'm reading. If there are any major howlers or ideas that spring to mind as you read, jot them down, but just keep going.

You may want to read it aloud, but you don't have to. That comes later. Just curl up with a cup of tea and a few custard creams and see what you think. Don't try to read it all at once. Try sections per day if it's easier. But do remember to be kind to yourself here. It's all too tempting to roll your eyes at some of the things you've said or repeated. Rather than berate yourself, embrace your achievements instead.

Stage 2: Adding in your research

During the shitty first draft, you may have included notes in your manuscript to remind yourself to complete the necessary research. Now's the time to do it. It might be a lot or it might just be the odd name for a quote you've used. Either way, get it done before you begin the actual editing process.

Stage 3: Structural editing

Now that you've read your first draft, you'll be in a great position to start making some of the major changes to the structure. If your outline was sound, you might not need to make big changes to the order of your chapters. Just check it flows in the way your reader needs it to. Does it take them in that logical order you were hoping for? Are you keeping your promise to the reader?

Be honest. It's better to make these changes now. You might also realise you've missed out something that needs adding in. Maybe it's a new chapter or maybe just a new subheading. Keep making notes as you go, either in your notebook or on your manuscript.

Within each chapter, check out the subheading order too. Do the sections flow in each chapter so your reader is taken on a mini journey in each one? Have you included all the action steps you want to? Are you moving the reader on in each chapter? It's also the time to check how the introduction and conclusion bookend your chapter.

Structure is important so take the time to really consider this stage. Often editors tell me that writers need support with this because it's integral to the reader's experience and enjoyment. Having said that, if there are any small structural changes to be made, your editor will point them out to you. Your beta readers will give you some much-needed insight too.

Stage 4: Copy editing

Copy editing is when you start to look at the finer details of your writing. You're checking for consistency and accuracy. So what do I mean by that?

Essentially you're looking for readability and whether you're repeating yourself with your word choices too frequently. As you read through your manuscript, you'll realise you favour certain words over others. Avoid repetition.

If you're repeating certain words, use the 'find and replace' tool if you're using Word. Look for those words within your manuscript and consider other words you could use instead.

Now is the time to cut the waffle too. Be as concise as possible. If you're labouring a point, cut it down. A copywriter friend of mine calls this 'trimming the fat'. He suggests cutting your words down by 20%. If you can say it in fewer words, do.

Finally, check for accuracy. Always write using words your audience will know and understand. If you're overly technical, it can be quite jarring for the reader. They don't want to stop midway through a sentence to dig out a thesaurus or type it into Google.

Double-check your choice of words too. The principle to adopt here is 'Don't do a Joey'. You know, that episode of *Friends* where Joey has to write a letter of recommendation to the adoption agency for Monica and Chandler? In an attempt to sound as intelligent as possible, he simply substitutes some words for those that sound more impressive, without checking the meaning in context.

Now I'm not saying you'd sign anything 'Baby Kangaroo Tribbiani', but you catch my drift. Keep your language simple. And when using synonyms, check for context. Keeping language simple and conversational makes the experience much nicer for your reader.

Stage 5: Proofreading

Imagine you're a teacher – chuck on a chunky knit and perch your glasses on the end of your nose if it helps. It's time to get your red pen out to check your work for spelling, punctuation and grammar errors. You'll also be able to catch any missing words too.

Now's the best time to read aloud. But do this in stages. Don't attempt to proofread all in one go. Take a few days and do a chapter or two per day. Circle any errors. If you're unsure of spellings, check them in a dictionary. It's okay if spelling isn't your forte, you've got plenty of other strengths. And yes, your editor will help you with this stage too.

Once you've done your proofread, it's time to do one more read through – and yes, out loud. Now before you throw something at me, bear with me. At this point of the process, you're probably ready to never look at your book again. You've read it so many times, you're seeing it in your sleep. I know.

But it's the final proofread before you send it off to your beta readers, so you'll want to double-check you're happy with it before you let it out of your sight. It's a bit like dropping your child off on their first day of school. You want them to have all the things they need before they skip merrily into the classroom. It's the same for your book.

Go through it once more and then leave it be. It's time for your beta readers to get their hands on it and give you some much-needed feedback. More on them in the next chapter.

Try not to procrastinate over this part. Just do it once. You'll be able to proofread it again (and again) before you hit 'publish'.

Stage 6: Deciding on your final title

Now's the time to consider your final title. Do your research here. What are the important keywords to include? In her book *How to Write Non-Fiction*, Joanna Penn gives the example of publishing a book called *Taking the Leap* and not selling many copies. She then changed the title to *Career Change: Stop hating your job, discover what you really want to do with your life, and start doing it.*

Much more descriptive, but the important words 'career change' are at the beginning of the title, so the book's more likely to be found in searches. My first book is called *Keeping Bums in Seats* – not something people are likely to search for. However, the tagline is 'The NQT's Guide to Behaviour Management'.

Keep keywords in mind when thinking of your title, but avoid 'keyword stuffing', otherwise your title will sound stilted. Do your research – what are the other titles out there in your niche? How are they using keywords? If you're unsure, poll your potential readers or ask those in your peer group for their suggestions.

Other things to consider

Editing will teach you a lot. Mainly how much you hate the sound of your own voice. But joking aside, going through it will make you a better writer; you'll also develop an intimate relationship with your book. You want (and need) to know it inside out. Take as much time as you need to. Especially if it's your first book.

Save each round of edits as a different draft number. It's very satisfying to see how it began as the shitty first draft, to how it looks when you finally type 'final draft' as the file name. It's a log of your writing journey and is definitely something you'll want to look back on.

It's helpful to print a fresh copy of your manuscript after each stage of editing, so that you're working with the most up-to-date version when you begin the next stage. This doesn't sit comfortably with some people, as it can seem like a waste of paper. I'll leave this up to you, of course. If you'd rather not, remember to change the font.

What do you need to put at the end of your book?

Use the end of your book wisely. It's a great place to showcase your services or website. It's also nice to start with acknowledgements to those who have supported you along the way. If you go on to write further books, you can use the back of your book to signpost readers to your entire catalogue.

Ask for reviews here too. Appeal to people's good nature and share how much it would mean to you. Reviews help the Amazon algorithm favour your book and put it in front of other potential readers too. If you're producing an ebook, you can add a review link to make the process as seamless as possible.

If you're thinking of adding a workbook or course to go alongside your book, include links to these here too.

Summary

Editing is an incredibly satisfying process. You're able to shape what you've created and mould it into something you feel proud of. Like with much of the writing process, you need to be in the right mindset to do it. It takes a lot out of you and it's all too easy to find fault with yourself.

Keep reminding yourself you're learning a new skill. When you first began to walk as a toddler, you didn't manage it on your first attempt. You fell down. A lot. Writing and editing are similar. We just find it much more frustrating because we're adults. We don't like falling down very much.

If and/or when you begin to feel frustrated, leave your manuscript for a day or two. Allow yourself time away. If it helps, keep to the writing habits you created to get the shitty first draft completed.

But most of all, remember you're going to get professional editing help. You're going to have an expert cast their eyes over and give you further support. Self-editing is just an opportunity to get it into the best shape that *you* can. It doesn't have to be perfect. A great editor will work with you to enhance it even more and to support you to make any other changes.

So grab a good cup of coffee, get your red pen out and have a go!

Action steps

1. Set yourself up with some habits to help you complete the editing process – maybe you'll keep the same writing time each day to get them done?
2. Complete each editing stage at your own pace – this isn't a race. It's an opportunity to make friends with your manuscript and really get to know it.
3. Reading aloud is the best way to get a feel for the flow and energy of the book. I can't recommend this enough. Lock yourself away if you need to, but do it you must.
4. Print a fresh copy of your manuscript after each round of edits – you can change the format so it looks like a book, saving your paper usage.
5. Professional editing will catch anything you've missed – do as much as you can and then leave it for them to look at.
6. Make your final decision on your book title – why not poll your audience on social media and see which option they prefer?

7. Always clean the loo before the cleaner comes. Better still, ask someone *else* to clean the loo before you clean the loo before the cleaner comes.

CHAPTER 10

WORKING WITH PROFESSIONALS

There's no such thing as a self-made man. You will reach your goals only with the help of others.

George Shinn

During World War One, a Chicago newspaper called Henry Ford an 'ignorant pacifist'. Ford sued the newspaper for libel. During the court proceedings, Ford himself was put on the stand so the newspaper's lawyers could show the world his apparent ignorance.

Throughout, the lawyers asked Ford a number of questions to demonstrate his lack of general knowledge. After a barrage of questioning, Ford became increasingly irritated, tired with having to prove himself.

After one particular question, he leant forward in his chair and pointed his finger at the lawyer, saying,

'If I should really want to answer the foolish question you've just asked me, let me remind you that I have a row of electric push-buttons on my desk and by pushing the right button, I can summon to my aid men who can answer any question I desire to ask. Now, will you kindly tell me why I should clutter up my mind with general knowledge for the purpose of being able to answer questions, when I have men around me who can supply any knowledge I require?'

The answer floored the lawyer. Hardly one of an ignorant man.

Likewise, American industrialist, Andrew Carnegie, openly said he had no knowledge of the technical side of the steel business. He simply hired people who did. He excelled in business; they excelled in steel production. Together they were unstoppable.

So I want you to adopt the Henry Ford and Andrew Carnegie approach. You don't need all the answers to writing, publishing, and launching your book. What you do need is your own team who can supply the knowledge and expertise you require. A team of professionals to get your book into the best shape possible.

If you've been following the editing process outlined in the previous chapter, your book is now in pretty good shape already. It's a great position to be in because the finish line is in sight. If you squint hard enough, you'll see someone waving a chequered flag.

I love all stages of writing, but this part is one of my favourites. Why? Because I get to work with some amazingly talented people. Professionals in their field who can work wonders with my manuscript and really make it shine. If you think your book was in pretty good shape before, you'll be amazed at what's about to be produced.

You may be wondering why you need to work with professionals. You're happy with how your book reads, so you should just hit 'publish', right?

No.

Now if I could drive over to wherever you live and plead with you on this next point, I would. If you're reading this outside the UK, I'd be willing to swim, which is pretty amazing as I've only got my 25m badge. It's so important; I'd buy some really good armbands.

If you're going down the traditional publishing route, rest assured your book will be edited to within an inch of its life by your publishing house. If, however, you're going down the self-publishing or 'indie author' route, you'll need to pull out your ear trumpet and listen.

It's imperative you work with professionals during the rest of your book-writing journey.

Readers can tell if a book is badly self-published. It sticks out like a DIY haircut your mum gave you as a child. You want to be as professional as possible. In my opinion, your reader shouldn't be able to tell if your book is self-published; the quality should be just as good as if it had been produced by a publishing house.

Have high expectations for your book. Even if you're doing an ebook to sell on your website, it's still important for it to look polished. You and your business' reputation are on the line and, while it won't ever be perfect, you want to get it as near as possible.

So if you're serious about giving your book a professional finish, read on.

Beta readers

Beta readers are people you'll approach before you send your book to a professional editor. They'll give you feedback on the content and the structure, so you can make any necessary changes to your work before your editor looks at it.

But who should be in your beta reader group?

You may feel nervous about sharing your work with others. Approach people you trust and whose feedback you'd like to receive.

A few words of caution here. Avoid asking people who are just going to pat you on the back and give you a gushing sentence about how brilliant you are. While that's lovely to hear, it's not going to help you too much at this point.

You want readers who are going to be honest. Readers who will give you constructive criticism, as well as pointing out things they liked. Ideally, your beta readers need to be members of your target audience. People who would buy the book in its finished form. Why? Because they'll give you feedback to improve your book even further and appeal to your readers even more. You could include someone who's at the same 'level' as you in your niche, so you can get feedback from a peer.

You don't need lots of beta readers. Approximately four should do it. When you give them your book to read, ask for specific feedback using questions such as:

- What did you think about the way this book is set out?
- Which features of the book did you particularly like?
- Who did you feel the book was aimed at?
- Were any sections unclear or confusing? What could I do to make them better?
- Were any sections particularly good? Why do you think that is?

Use the feedback to help make further improvements to your manuscript. You don't have to adopt all the suggestions, of course, but if something repeatedly comes up as an area for improvement, it's usually worth considering it. If anything is deemed as 'unclear', take a second look.

Using beta readers from your target audience works because their opinions really make the difference. Giving your book to someone who would never read it in the first place will give you feedback that isn't helpful at all.

You shouldn't pay for beta readers, but showing an element of appreciation is always nice! You can send them a free copy when it's published or thank them in your acknowledgements.

Editors

After you've made the changes from your beta read, you're ready to send your work to your editor. You may feel apprehensive about this, but I promise you it's a process you'll actually come to enjoy. A lot of it comes down to finding an editor who feels right for you. Someone you feel comfortable with and 'gets' your book.

Often, editors will specialise in working on certain types of books, even if it's just non-fiction. As with any potential partnership, speak to a few different editors until you find one who understands your book and your message. Recommendations are useful here, as you want to work with someone who has a good reputation.

Your editor should take your book through the three stages of the editing process: structural, copy and line editing, although not all non-fiction editors offer structural advice. The less structural editing you need, the better. Another reason your beta readers come into their own.

Editors don't make changes for you. They simply suggest what you could do to improve your book. You don't have to take on their recommendations if you don't want to – but I strongly recommend you consider everything they suggest. If you're traditionally published, you may have less say in what you need to change.

Your relationship with your editor should be two-way. Improve your book as a team. Try not to be too defensive about your work. Yes, you've put your heart and soul into the process, but don't let emotions get the better of you. An editor is coming at this impartially, which is worth its weight in gold. The more you work together, the better your book will be.

And finally, don't forget to contact an editor early on. If they have a long waiting list, it's usually a good sign.

Editors vary in price, according to experience. You'll usually send them an approximate word count so they can give you a rough estimate of how much it will cost. They may ask for a sample chapter to look at, but that does vary depending on the editor. Some offer sample edits too. You're likely to spend upwards of £350 on editing, depending on the length of your manuscript.

Proofreaders

Once you've gone through all the editing stages, you may wish to ask your beta readers to take another look, but it's not essential. You'll need time to make any revisions your editor suggested and then your book will be in its best shape yet.

Proofreaders are the final pair of eyes on your book before it goes to publication. They're checking for any small errors. Many editors are also proofreaders, so you could stick with the same person or hire someone else to get another pair of eyes on it.

If your editor also offers proofreading services, they could offer an editing/proofreading bundle for a cheaper cost than paying for the two separately. Price for proofreading is dependent on word count – £10 to £15 per 1,000 words is about average.

Cover designers

People judge books by their covers, as much as they claim they don't. I do it. You do it. We all do it. Your front cover is like your elevator pitch. It needs to get your reader's attention for all the right reasons and look the business. If it looks shite, people will run a mile. They won't even pick it up. Harsh, but true.

Not all graphic designers are able to produce covers. It's often an area they specialise in. Again, look for recommendations. Why not check out the covers of some of the indie books you've read or seen out on the market? All authors will have at least credited the cover designer on the inside cover, if not in the acknowledgements. Looking at other cover designs you like also helps you when discussing ideas with a designer – they'll often ask if there are any you've seen that you like the style of.

Another option is looking at websites such as 99designs.com. You create a design brief and then experienced cover designers pitch their ideas to you. Prices start at £240 and go all the way up to £949. It's quite a simple process and they guide you through the brief-writing process so you get exactly what you want. You've also got websites such as upwork.com or fiverr.com where you can find freelancers willing to design your cover.

You can choose an 'off the shelf' cover from websites such as thebookcoverdesigner.com – once they've sold that cover, it's not available again, so you can be sure yours will be unique to you. Prices start from as little as £30. It won't look as refined, but if it's just for an ebook, it's quite a good option. You'll just need some patience to find the better designs among some truly bizarre ones!

Try not to do a DIY cover design if you can possibly help it – not even using Canva. It's tempting but it's very obvious you've done it yourself. If you're putting together a short PDF ebook, you *might* get away with it, but even then I'd still try and get some simple graphic design work done so it looks as polished as possible.

It's always fun to get your audience involved in choosing your cover design – and it'll build up the hype around your book's release. When you have a couple of designs to choose from, why not ask them to vote for their favourite? It can really help with raising their excitement at the prospect of your book being ready.

Formatters

If you're preparing your book for a digital platform such as Amazon, you'll need your book to be properly formatted. It's not as simple as uploading a word document. You can format your own books with Vellum software or use the templates provided by Kindle or Draft2Digital, which are downloadable.

If you want to avoid the hassle, you can outsource this process to someone who knows what they're doing. You'll find plenty of experienced people on fiverr.com who can do this quite cheaply.

You'll also need it formatted for print too. Only send your book to be formatted once it's completely signed off and ready to go. It's the very final stage before publishing.

Reviewers

It's worth getting what Joanna Penn affectionately calls your 'street team' in place. Part of your team will be your beta readers. As well as giving you feedback on the early stages of your book, you can also approach them to write reviews for launch week.

Give out some early copies to a review team too. Use some of your superfans or trusted members of your audience for this. I'm sure you can think of a few people. Why not invite people on your email list to volunteer for the role? Try to recruit about ten people.

Give them pre-release copies and ask them to write an honest review on Amazon once release day comes. You can use their reviews on social media as part of your launch week or on your website. Reviewers on Amazon must declare they were given a copy for review purposes, but you see that quite often so it's nothing unusual.

A good number of reviews on Amazon helps the algorithm put your book in front of more people. The 'magic number' is often cited as fifty, but obviously that's not a number you need to try and get to before launch week ... or even beyond it.

Summary

Working with professionals is the final step towards publication. It's an exciting time, but also one that requires planning and coordination on your part. If you work with a virtual assistant, you could outsource it to them to deal with, but I do urge you to meet with editors and cover designers yourself, even for the initial brief.

Try to take the emotion out of this process and put yourself in the shoes of your reader. It's all about them, after all. Take feedback and suggestions as guidance that will make the book more helpful to your readers.

You don't have to go through such a big editing process if you're doing a quick ebook for your website, but I do suggest using beta readers and proofreaders as a bare minimum, even for PDFs. You want your book to be in line with your brand and the professional values it holds.

Keep your audience involved for this part of the journey too – it begins to warm them up for your release date and launch process.

Once it all comes together, you're ready for the most exciting part of this whole process: publication and launch. We'll be diving into all that good stuff in the next chapter.

Action steps

1. Get booked in with all professionals as early as possible.
2. Do as much self-editing as you can before sending it to your beta readers.
3. Ask your beta readers specific questions about your book, rather than just hoping for general feedback. Use their answers to improve it where possible.

4. Work with an editor to make your book shine – get onto discovery calls with a few of them to see who seems a good fit. Use recommended editors where possible.
5. Avoid creating your own cover design – there are lots of options out there so investigate based on your budget.
6. Once you've had your book proofread, send it out to your street team to get those early reviews in place, ready for launch week and your website.
7. Hire formatters to prepare your book for digital publishing or for print, or both.
8. Keep your reader at the forefront of your decisions – this book is for them, so put some emotional distance between you and your book when working with professionals.
9. Work at a desk with push buttons. Summon anything, from professional help to biscuits.

CHAPTER 11

PUBLISHING YOUR BOOK

Publishing a book is like being pregnant. By the end you're just ready to get the baby out.

Carmen DeSousa

'And ever since Rabbit and Miss Bee, I've wanted to be a writer, though I rarely told anyone so.'

So said JK Rowling, after describing a childhood where she would often make up stories to tell her sister. Can you imagine if she'd never followed through on that desire? Never put pen to paper? Whether you're a *Harry Potter* fan or not, you can't argue it's not had a profound impact on the world of fiction.

But it took Jo Rowling guts to try and publish her book. She'd spent more than five years planning, researching and writing *The Philosopher's Stone*. It was then rejected by twelve publishers until it finally found a home at Bloomsbury. Even so, her advance was £2,500, and with a small print-run.

It's a common theme among writers who submit their work to agents and publishers for consideration. For every 'yes' or 'maybe', you've heard 'no' a hundred times. As Carmen DeSousa says in the quote above, you just want to get your book out there after working on it for so long. It's challenging when you've got more hurdles to jump over.

But you're in a better position than JK Rowling was back in 1996. There are fewer hoops to jump through when self-publishing your work. Yes, you've got lots to do in this part of the writing process, but it's far more straightforward.

The publication process

You've done all the hard work and now it's time to finally publish your book. It's exciting and daunting all at the same time. It's important not to rush this stage though. Give yourself time and space to do it right. You'll find all the handy hints and tips you need in the following pages.

In this chapter, we'll look at the different types of publishing and what your options are. I won't go into great detail about how exactly you need to upload things – all popular digital platforms have plenty of videos and guides to help you. It's not complicated. Just take it slowly and follow the guidance carefully. If you're unsure of anything, they have support options in place to help you.

Much of this chapter is aimed at people who want to self-publish their work. Even if you're on the traditional publishing path, it's still worth reading on because you may wish to self-publish in the future.

Publication is often the most daunting part of writing your book. Up until now, only a select few people have read your work, people you know and trust. Putting it out for anyone's eyes takes things up a notch. It's about powering on through when you feel the butterflies in your stomach.

You're not going to please everyone with your work, nor should you try to. When your mouse is hovering over the 'publish' button, try not to pause or freak out. This is a perfect time to practise Mel Robbins' '5 second rule'. Count back to zero and just do it.

You've done as much preparation as you can. You don't need to 'just read it once more' to check. Your readers want to read it. Change those feelings of fear into feelings of excitement. You're stepping into such an exciting space, so take a deep breath and go.

So whatever your next publication steps are, strap yourself in. We're on the final leg of your writing journey and it's the most exciting and important stage. It's time to get your book out into the world and into the hands of your expectant readers.

Publishing

When you think of self-publishing, you may only be aware of two main options. One is publishing your book on your website; the other is Amazon. It's not surprising really, as it holds 50% of all book distribution. You can easily just publish on Amazon and be done with it. But it's worth exploring other options too.

Publishing to your website

You can publish your book straight to your website. The easiest way to do this is with a PDF. However, it's not the greatest reading experience for your audience. You may get some who are happy to download and print your ebook as a PDF. Indeed, my husband often does this when reading about nutrition and exercise programmes.

But I think it's worth selling it as an ePub copy too. This will enable people to read it on their devices, in the same format as an ebook from Amazon or other digital publishing platforms.

One of the great benefits is you earn 100% of the royalties. You're in complete control of the process and you can add new chapters or change the cover quickly and easily.

But you'll need to consider that Amazon works like a search engine. If people are searching for books in your niche, Amazon will include yours in that general search. If you *only* sell it on your website, you're missing out on potential exposure from the algorithms on digital publishing platforms.

Amazon Kindle Direct Publishing (KDP)

The largest platform to self-publish your work, Amazon has refined the process to make it as easy as possible for you. Once you've had your book properly formatted, with a cover design that fits the Amazon dimensions, it's just a matter of uploading it. You'll find plenty of information online about how to do this, including from Amazon itself, so spend a bit of time understanding the process before you upload.

You can be part of KDP Select, which is a free ninety-day programme to promote your book exclusively on Amazon. When you choose to enrol your book in KDP Select, you're committing to make the digital format of that book available exclusively through KDP. You can't distribute your book digitally anywhere else, including on your website. However, you can distribute your book in physical format or audio.

Other digital platforms

If you decide not to exclusively publish with KDP Select, you can sell your book on some of the smaller digital platforms too. Here are a few of the more popular ones:

- Kobo
- IngramSpark
- Draft2Digital

Each platform is slightly different, but most accept the ePub format. As well as Amazon, I publish my books on Draft2Digital, Apple iBooks and Smashwords. Each one has similar royalty payments to Amazon so it's worth getting your book onto as many different platforms as possible.

Publishing print copies

You may wish to publish print copies of your books too. It's such a thrill to hold a copy of your own book in your hands. You can also sell physical copies at events you attend or at speaking engagements. You may also like to do giveaways or send copies as thank-you gifts to clients etc.

Again, Amazon makes this easy for you. Before print on demand, self-published authors had to do a print-run of copies and store them to send out by hand. Now, however, print on demand means you don't need physical copies of your books in storage. When someone orders your book on Amazon, it's printed and shipped to them straight away. If they have Amazon Prime, it can be in their hands the following day.

It's your print copies that need to look professional. As long as you have a good quality cover design, Amazon prints things to a high standard. You can even order test copies to check for quality.

Once you've set up your KDP account with Amazon, uploading your formatted manuscript for print copies is straightforward. You'll find plenty of advice on how to do this online – Amazon gives step-by-step instructions too.

Audio books

A growing number of indie authors are choosing to publish their work to audio. It's just another way to get people to enjoy your work. I listen to books on dog walks or when I'm on a long car journey. It's the same for a lot of people, particularly when they're commuting and want to use that time to improve an area of their life.

It's getting easier to share your book to an audio platform, with the most popular platforms being Audible, ACX (owned by Amazon) and Findaway Voices. You'll need to consider who you'd like to narrate your book. Some authors enjoy doing this process themselves, others prefer to hire voice talent to do it for them. Either way, you'll need to factor in the cost of your time or a professional's, as well as hiring a studio to record in.

Just as people judge books by their covers, others will judge the sound quality of your audio book. Unfortunately, recording it under a duvet in your garden shed won't cut it.

Recording studios don't have to be expensive. You can find local ones that you can hire at reasonable prices. You'll then have all the equipment you need. Once your book has been recorded, get it professionally edited too.

Summary

Deciding when and how to publish your book is an important part of the process. You need to have a clear idea in your mind of what this will look like for you personally. While it's worth looking at how other people in your niche have published their books, always stick with what feels right for you. Just because audio books are popular, doesn't mean you need to do an audio version of yours.

If you want to keep things simple, using KDP on Amazon is probably the best option. You can then investigate further options in the future, should you wish to. But if you've got time to investigate all the options thoroughly, you'll be able to get your book into the hands of more readers.

If you don't want to learn how to self-publish your book, there are companies out there who'll do it for you. You need to be careful here and only go with reputable companies, but you can find those, like BookBaby, who will help you with editing, formatting and publishing your book. Check out the Alliance of Independent Authors website as it provides guidance/information on finding professionals to work with.

Once your book is ready for publication, it's time to think about the launch strategy you want to put in place, as well as other marketing strategies for the future. We'll cover all that in the next chapter.

Action steps

1. Decide where you're going to publish your book – look at all the possible options and see what feels right for you and your readers
2. Investigate all types of publishing – from ebook to print to audio. You can outsource the more technical bits too, so look at freelancing websites such as Fiverr and Upwork.
3. Avoid procrastinating over hitting the 'publish' button – once your book is in good shape, it's time to launch it into the world.
4. Press 'publish'! And then do a little dance/drink a litre of wine/run around the house naked.

CHAPTER 12

LAUNCHING AND MARKETING YOUR BOOK

If writing and publishing a book is like giving birth to a child, book marketing is like rearing it.

Heather Hart

Christine Ohuruogu is one of the best female 400m runners Team GB has ever had. She is the former Olympic, World and Commonwealth champion. Despite a shaky start to her career, Christine blossomed into a formidable athlete, staying at the top of her game for over eight years.

While it's natural to admire such a consummate athlete, it's her racing style I loved watching. For most of her races, Christine never really led from the front. She'd stay in the middle of the pack, pushing herself to stay in the mix and showing amazing stamina and strength.

But it was the end of the race where Christine would come into her own. When many other 400m athletes began to 'travel backwards' as their muscles tired out with lactate build-up, Christine would surge forward, often pipping them on the line to win the race. Indeed, some of her greatest victories were won in this way, with me staring in disbelief at her final burst of strength.

Writing a book is similar to a 400m race. You work hard for the duration of the 'race' but if your race tactics aren't quite right, you end up too exhausted to make it over the finish line. As good training in the winter months helps athletes win medals in the summer events, taking care to plan the launch of your book will do wonders for you when it's time to get it into the hands of your eager readers.

Launching

It's easy to think that the hard work is over once your book is finished. You hit publish and sit back, waiting for the royalties and sales to come in. Time to put your feet up, right?

Erm ... no.

As a business owner, you know things really don't work that way. Hitting publish is a big achievement and one you should feel proud of, but you need to embrace the idea that your book is part of an ongoing journey. You can't expect to just put it out into the world and see it sell automatically.

If you want it to sell, if you want it to grow your business, you'll need to invest time and energy into your launch and marketing plan. It's one of the reasons I suggest bringing your audience on your writing journey from the start. You're slowly building the excitement and the hype for your book. It's easier to launch something to a group of excited and eager readers than pitching it cold.

Your launch process is far easier if you're selling to a group of people who are eager to buy. By putting the following ideas and strategies into place, you'll have a long line of people ready to buy your book.

If you've opted to go with a traditional publisher, ideas for launching and marketing will still be relevant to you. Many publishing houses look for authors to do much of the leg work when it comes to this side of the publishing process, so it's great to have a plan in place.

Unfortunately, you can't rely on your publisher to do it for you, particularly if you're a relatively unknown author. Only the big names have large marketing and launch budgets behind them.

So this chapter will take you from creating a launch strategy to ongoing marketing plans. One of the many great things about writing a book is its capacity to grow your business in so many different ways. We'll explore this too.

So let's get launching.

Bringing your audience on your publication journey

Before you consider your launch, how can you prepare your audience for your book as early as possible?

As you should know by now, I firmly believe that an audience you've established, be it on social media or via email, should be part of this journey. We're a nosey species by nature, so we love following what others are doing. You can use this to your advantage.

Within your audience, you'll have what entrepreneur and author Pat Flynn calls 'superfans'. These are a group of people who share, buy and engage with everything you do. They're your brand advocates, recommending you to others. You may only have a couple of advocates, but if you're an established coach or consultant, you'll know who they are.

You may even be a superfan of someone you admire yourself; I know I am.

So it's time to get these superfans on board. Depending on your relationship with them, ask a few of them to be in your street team or launch crew. Launching your book can feel daunting, so having a team around you gives you the boost you need.

If you have an email list, announce your intention to write a book in your weekly newsletter. Give people updates on social media about how it's going. Share photos of you in your writing space or hitting some of your milestone markers. Wave your red pen at the camera during the editing process or ask your audience/followers to vote for your book cover. All of these add to the hype, priming your audience to be potential buyers.

As I've mentioned before, it can feel scary to put yourself out there like that, to be vulnerable and courageous. But you'll soon realise that people want to support you. They want to encourage you and embrace your creativity. So only share what you feel comfortable sharing, but *do* share some parts of your journey. You'll feel the love and support if you do.

Launch planning

During the planning stages, I invited you to consider your publication date in advance, to give yourself a deadline to work towards. But it also gives you an opportunity to think about how and when you want to start your launch process.

Now, if you've ever launched a product or service for your business, you'll know a launch can be exhausting. It's best to plan it out in advance. One good thing is that your book then becomes part of your evergreen model. It's not something you need to keep relaunching. Once it's out there in the world, it can then become part of your regular marketing strategy.

So with that in mind, you can build a launch plan that really propels your book out there at the initial stages. Ideally you need to start talking about your book launch about 4–6 weeks before publication date, to give you enough time to warm up your audience to the event.

It's up to you how you do this, but launching can include promotional offers, speaking at public events/on podcasts etc., writing guest blogs, virtual/in-person launch parties, offering discounts to bulk buyers and getting reviews on your Amazon page. Build a launch team to help you spread the word. They can help write reviews too. Just be sure you check out Amazon's guidance and comply with their review rules.

If you want an example of a great launch plan, head on over to Lucy Werner's Instagram page, where you'll see how she prepared for the launch of her second book, *Brand Yourself*. A brilliant strategy expertly put in place, all the while ensuring people ordered their copies ... with smiles on their faces.

Like any launch, give it the time and energy this sort of thing requires. It will be exhausting but worth it. Just ensure you leave enough time for launching successfully. Springing a book upon your audience just won't work.

If, however, it's a freebie you're offering as part of your sales funnel, your launch won't need to be as long. It's one of the reasons that, during the initial planning stages, I encourage you to think about why you're publishing your book. When you know what the reason is and the outcome you want, the launch process becomes easier to plan.

Finally, keep things realistic for you. Only you know what you can manage. Be kind to yourself if your launch doesn't fully go to plan. Just do as much as you can and continue to feel proud of your achievement. You'll have plenty of opportunities to continue to promote your book after the launch date.

Creating a marketing plan

Marketing plans aren't going to be new to you, but it's worth thinking about how your book is going to fit into yours. Your launch plan will probably be a separate document to your marketing plan, but once your book is out there in the world, I suggest you make your book a regular feature.

One of the things I love about books is how evergreen they are. You can use their content in so many different ways. You can take an element of a chapter and turn it into a blog post. Or you can take one subheading and break it down into social media posts. By referencing your book in many different ways, you'll continue to see sales, months and years after you publish.

Once the initial launch phase is over, add your book to your overall marketing plan. You can then look at and review it each month or quarter. You've put all this hard work into creating a brilliant piece of work; it would be a shame if you let things fall by the wayside.

Lots of business owners use books as entry points to their sales funnel. If they're not giving it away as a freebie in exchange for an email address, they're using it as a low-ticket offer within their funnel. Sometimes as a tripwire offer after someone signs up for their freebie. Think about how your book fits into your bigger business model.

One thing that's worked for me in the past is to use social media to regularly market my books. I'll dedicate one post per week with some content linked to the book – whether it's an educational piece from my book to encourage people to buy it, or simply a promo post telling people about it. Just keep talking about it, even after the initial launch period has worn off.

If you want your book to keep doing good things for your business, keep talking about it. When I interviewed Lucy Werner on my Instagram video series, she noted how sales for her books would decrease as soon as she stopped talking about them. It just goes to show how quickly things can fade from people's minds.

Here are some marketing tips to help you continue to promote your book:

- On Instagram, take one concept from your book and turn it into a grid post, a video, a reel or a carousel. Next month, take the same concept and do a different type of post you haven't done before. Repurposing wins!
- Include reviews for your book regularly on social media. Tag the person so they'll share it too.
- Create a hashtag for your book that people can use and turn on notifications for. You'll then see when someone uses it and can then share that with your followers.
- Ask people to take photos when they're reading your book – Sarah Townsend, author of *Survival Skills for Freelancers*, does this really well. She then shares these photos on social media.
- Run competitions to win copies of your book – ask winners to leave a review and share it on their social media.
- Run book sales at different times of the year – leading up to Christmas is always a good one. You can change the price of your book on Amazon for periods of time to go alongside these sales promotions.

From your marketing plan, you'll probably have lots more ideas. Just be consistent with your approach and you'll soon see how evergreen your book becomes.

Using your book for PR opportunities

Your book is a wonderful PR piece, opening up so many different doors for you. It doesn't have to be during your launch period either, although PR opportunities will play an important role here too.

A brilliant book to help with any kind of PR is *Hype Yourself* by Lucy Werner. You can take much of the advice in it and apply it to your book launch.

Here are a few ideas to get you started:

- Find podcasts that would be interested in your niche topic – you'll often get the opportunity to promote your book at the end of it, reaching an even wider audience.
- Look out for possible speaking engagements – you can base a talk around the content of your book, which will entice people to buy it once the talk is over. Take a box of books with you, so people can buy a copy once they've heard you speak.
- Approach popular blogs for guest posting opportunities – successful blogs are often seeking people to guest post. You can pitch a blog post linked to your book's content and promote it in your 'about the author' section at the bottom.

You'll find that PR is an important part of your launch strategy, as you'll want to get as many people pre-ordering and talking about your book as possible. But it doesn't have to stop there. Much like your marketing plan, your book can become an integral part of your business PR plan too. It's great to have it in your back pocket as something to offer.

Other post-publication possibilities

Once your book is out in the world, you may want to think about other ways it can build and grow your business. You may find people will ask for alternative ways of working with you or getting hold of the book's information.

These include:

- Workshops – people want to put the action steps from a book into practice but struggle to find the time or accountability to do it. You could run regular workshops linked to your book so people can take their understanding further.

- Masterclasses – this is another excellent way to promote your book. Link your masterclass to your book and use the event to invite people to purchase it.
- Online courses – more and more people are running online courses to accompany their books, using chapters as modules. Upload your content to one of the many hosting sites out there and you could soon have another stream of passive income from your book. It's quite a bit of work initially, recording the modules, but you've got all the content planned out. Your action steps can even form the course activities.
- Workbooks – another growing area in post-publication. You can create and sell a workbook that puts all your action steps together. I've seen this from some of the biggest names in the business, so if they can do it, so can you.
- Consulting and mentoring – brands and individuals want to work with the best; they want to work with specialists. With a book under your belt, you can begin to establish a consulting business off the back of it. You're often able to charge higher rates as a published author too. Something Lucy Werner shared during her chat with me on 'Happy Writers Live!'.
- Speaking engagements – yes, these can be a part of PR, but you may find people want to book you as a keynote speaker, particularly if your book covers a really interesting topic or niche, or if your story is particularly inspiring or different.
- Other books within the series – now I know you've only just finished your book, but you may find that ideas for other books start to play around in your head. If it's something you'd like to pursue, you can always create a series of books to grow your business even further.

Keep in mind that opportunities will crop up you won't even have considered. Try not to get overwhelmed by this. Take on what you wish to pursue and decline others that don't really float your boat. You don't have to do everything.

If you're introverted, you may find some of these too overwhelming. As with everything in business, keep things manageable and, most of all, keep them enjoyable. If you don't enjoy a particular aspect of marketing or promoting your book, don't do it. Build your book into your business in a way that's right for you.

Summary

Writing a book doesn't end when you hit 'publish'. It's an ongoing process and should be part of your business strategy moving forward. But whatever your plans, they must make you happy. If you're not someone who enjoys being on camera, there are plenty of other ways to promote your book that don't require showing your face. If writing your book has put you off writing guest blog posts for a while, do something else.

But do have a plan. It would be such a shame if your book, the one you've put so much into, flops because of poor planning. I tend to think about this stage when I've done the first draft and I'm having a bit of time away from my manuscript. I then know what lies ahead and feel far more prepared for it.

The most important thing to remember during this part is to have your street team on board. You'll rely on them to get you through the busy launch period and beyond. But once the word gets out about your book, once people start recommending it to their friends, things will really pick up speed.

So be consistent, have plans in place and most importantly, enjoy it.

Action steps

1. Consider how you can bring your audience on this journey with you – establish who your book fans are and how they can help you.
2. Create a launch plan well in advance – allow 4–6 weeks to really get things rolling and for the excitement to build.
3. Add your book to your annual/quarterly/monthly marketing plans – you'll need to continue promoting it on a regular basis.
4. Look at how your book can feature in your PR plans – create a new one if necessary that's just linked to your book. Having a separate PR strategy for your launch will be really helpful too.
5. Get some ideas together for how your book could evolve in the future – maybe a course or a workshop? Are there any other books up your sleeve? You'll need a well-earned break from writing once you're published and launched. But it's always worth bearing these things in mind.
6. Channel your inner Christine Ohuruogu and don some Lycra during events - if it all goes tits up, you can escape with haste.

SUMMARY

Who you are tomorrow begins with what you do today.

Tim Fargo

You've made it! What a huge achievement and one you should feel so very proud of.

When you achieve something as momentous as writing and publishing a book, take the time to celebrate what you've done.

Sometimes, as business owners, we head straight into the next thing without pausing to take a breath and realise what we've achieved. If writing a book has been a lifelong dream of yours, it's even sweeter.

It's always worth reflecting on what you've done to get to this point too. What have you learned about yourself? What habits did you enjoy? Which parts of the process did you find hard and why? Would you do it again and if so, what would you do differently?

The first time I ever wrote 'The End' on a first draft, I burst into tears. It had been months of hard work, of doubting myself, of almost giving up. Typing those words signified a new me. Someone who could do hard things and overcome obstacles. I couldn't quite believe I'd done it. It changed how I viewed myself and gave me so much confidence to continue to write.

If you've had similar feelings during this process, please know you're not alone. This may be my sixth book, but doubt and overwhelm have crept in here and there. No one is impervious to it. It's about ploughing on regardless. It's about 'feeling the fear and doing it anyway', as author Susan Jeffers wrote.

I'm so excited for you, to see where this book takes you and the opportunities it presents to you. I hope, like me, it's given you a new-found sense of confidence and self-belief. Not only in your ability to face a challenge, but in your message and in your brand. In the work you're trying to do to transform people's lives.

All that's left for me to say is good luck. I hope your book grows your business and gets your message out there to everyone who needs it. I hope it gives you opportunities you'd never imagined and gives you the confidence to face challenges head on, knowing you've done what many people try to do and never achieve.

Releasing your work into the world often feels daunting. You're opening yourself up to the judgement and opinions of others. Don't let that stop you. Grab this opportunity with both hands and go out into the arena with your head held high. Be vulnerable. Be courageous. Be badass.

As Brené Brown said:

When I see people stand fully in their truth, or when I see someone fall down, get back up, and say, 'Damn. That really hurt, but this is important to me and I'm going in again'—my gut reaction is, 'What a badass.'

Your book is your legacy. Now go out there and own it.

I dare you.

BIBLIOGRAPHY

Briles, Judith (2013) *Snappy, Sassy, Salty: Wise Words for Authors and Writers,* Mile High Press

Brown, Brené (2015) *Rising Strong*, Vermilion

Butler, Octavia (2005) *Blood Child and Other Stories,* Seven Stories Press

Caswell, Stephanie (2015) *Keeping Bums in Seats: The NQT's Guide to Behaviour Management,* Createspace Independent Publishing

Csíkszentmihályi, Mihaly (2002) *Flow: The Classic Work on How to Achieve Happiness,* Penguin Random House

DeSousa, Carmen (2013) *Carmen DeSousa's Blog, page 45,* Goodreads.com

Doyle, Glennon (2020) *Untamed: Stop Pleasing, Start Living,* Vermilion

Dweck, Carol (2017) *Mindset: Changing the Way You Think to Fulfil Your Potential*, Little, Brown

Elrod, Hal (2017) *The Miracle Morning: The 6 Habits That Will Transform Your Life Before 8am*, John Murray Press

Fargo, Tim (2014) *Alphabet Success: Keeping it Simple - My Secrets to Success,* Createspace Independent Publishing

Fogg, BJ (2019) *Tiny Habits: The Small Changes that Change Everything*, Ebury Publishing

Forleo, Marie (2019) *Everything is Figureoutable: How One Simple Belief Can Help Us Overcome Any Obstacle and Create Unstoppable Success*, Penguin Books

Gilbert, Elizabeth (2015) *Big Magic: Creative Living Beyond Fear,* Bloomsbury Publishing

Gladwell, Malcolm (2008) *Outliers: The Story of Success*, Penguin Books

Hardy, Darren (2010) *The Compound Effect: Jumpstart Your Income, Your Life, Your Success,* Hachette Books

Holiday, Ryan (2015) *The Obstacle is the Way: The Ancient Art of Turning Adversity into Advantage*, Profile

Jeffers, Susan (2007) *Feel the Fear and Do It Anyway,* Vermilion

Kanter, Rosabeth (2014) Twitter, August 1st 2014, @rosabethkanter

King, Stephen (2000) *On Writing: A Memoir of the Craft*, Hodder and Stoughton

Lamott, Anne (1994) *Bird by Bird: Some Instructions on Writing and Life*, Canongate Books

McGill, Bryant (2018) *Simple Reminders: Inspiration for Living Your Best Life*, Independent

McKeown, Greg (2014) *Essentialism: The Disciplined Pursuit of Success*, Ebury Publishing

McKeown, Greg (2021) *Effortless: Make it Easier to Do What Matters Most*, Ebury Publishing

McKeown, Greg, (2020) How to Achieve Your Goals Effortlessly with Greg McKeown, *Feel Better Live More Podcast*, Episode #183

Penn, Joanna (2013) *Career Change: Stop Hating Your Job, Discover What You Really Want to Do With Your Life and Start Doing It*, Createspace Independent Publishing

Penn, Joanna (2018) *How to Write Non-Fiction: Turn Your Knowledge into Words*, Curl Up Press

Robbins, Mel (2017) *The 5 Second Rule: The Surprisingly Simple Way to Live, Love and Speak with Courage*, Post Hill Press

Shinn, George (2013) *The Miracle of Motivation: The Guide to Becoming Everything You Want to Be*, Shinn Publishing

Sincero, Jen (2018) *You Are a Badass at Making Money: Master the Mindset of Wealth*, John Murray Press

Smith, Zadie (2014) 'Zadie Smith On the Psychology of The Two Types of Writers', themarginalian.org

Townsend, Sarah (2020) *Survival Skills for Freelancers: Tried and Tested Tips to Help You Ace Self-Employment Without Burnout*, Sarah Townsend

Werner, Lucy (2020) *Hype Yourself: A No-Nonsense PR Toolkit for Small Businesses,* Practical Inspiration Publishing

Werner, Lucy and Chatelet, Hadrien (2021) *Brand Yourself: A No-Nonsense Brand Toolkit for Small Businesses*, Practical Inspiration Publishing

ACKNOWLEDGEMENTS

One of my favourite parts of any non-fiction book is reading the acknowledgements - I don't know why, but there's something curious about who a writer chooses to thank when they've finished their work.

First and foremost, I'm going to thank myself. Arrogant? Crazy? Narcissistic? Quite possibly. But I've come to think of it in a different way. All my work on personal development has led me to understand how important it is to be kind to yourself - as kind as you are to others. We're often our own worst critics and I'm doing my best to put a stop to it. So I want to thank myself for sitting down in the chair everyday, especially when the summer sun was calling and I really did want to be outside with a gin. I'm proud of what I've achieved and I think I deserve to pat myself on the back. After all, what better way to live up to my values of self-care and self-love? Glennon Doyle and Brené Brown - thank you. You've helped me see how important it is. And my inner critic? Elizabeth Gilbert was right, you did enjoy coming along for the ride, didn't you? Shame you couldn't pitch your tent anywhere safe ...

A huge thank you to my editor, Jessica. I couldn't have asked for a better person to take care of my book and shape it into something I'm truly proud of. You are exceptional at what you do and I can't wait to work with you again on the next one. A big thank you to my proofreader, Bernadette, too - your sharp eye caught all those little errors and tightened things up nicely.

A big hug and thank you to my cover designer, Rachel. Who'd have thought all those years ago in Mr Wright's maths class, you'd be designing the cover of my book? I'm thrilled we got to work on this together and I'm always amazed at how awesomely talented you are.

My street team! You were such a huge help with beta reading and feedback. Big thanks to Shona, Jenny, Jill and Katie - all of you were kind enough to tell me the bits you loved and the bits that needed work. It's a better book because of it. I'm also glad the story with Goldie brought about so many laughs - she'll be thrilled!

To my Happy Writers community, particularly on Instagram and in my Facebook group. I have got to know so many of you since starting my business and you've all been so supportive and kind. A special thank you to Sarah Townsend, Lucy Werner, Shona Chambers and Jacqueline Kent for sharing your wisdom on Happy Writers Live!

Big love to my wonderful friend, Kay. Not a day goes by that I don't feel grateful for our friendship. You're like a sister to me and I couldn't do half the things I do without your unwavering support. Thank you for *everything.*

To my mum, dad and two wonderful sisters - you're all marvellous. Special thanks to Naomi and Aaron (and Goldie) for giving me such a funny story to tell.

And finally to Family Caz. Ben and Beau, you're the reason I do this. I want to show you that you can do anything you want in life. Just have courage and faith ... and don't be afraid to make mistakes! It's how you'll learn. Yes you may drive me nuts with the continuous wrestling, but you also make me insanely proud.

Paul, it's quite an amazing thing, you know, spending every day with your best friend. Someone who supports you wholeheartedly in everything you do. And that's what I'm lucky enough to experience with you by my side. Thank you for believing in me and loving me so completely. Now if you could just hang the washing in the way I want you to, we'd be golden ...

ABOUT THE AUTHOR

Steph Caswell started her career as a teacher, reaching the lofty heights of deputy headship, before she saw sense and started her own writing business. She now works as a writing coach, supporting female entrepreneurs to write brilliant books in their niche.

She's the author of six books, including three books for early career teachers. She's also worked as a ghostwriter on two personal development books for an Australian publisher. *Dare to Write* is Steph's sixth book.

She lives in Surrey with her husband, Paul, and two children. When she's not typing away, you can find her walking her dog, Flo, or spending hours in a stationery shop gazing at the notebooks, pretending she can't see Paul tapping his watch.

Connect with Steph

Website: stephcaswell.com

Instagram: @creatinghappywriters

Facebook: www.facebook.com/creatinghappywriters

Email: steph@stephcaswell.com

Printed in Dunstable, United Kingdom

82132854R00077